ANTIQUES
OF THE AIR
MICHAEL F JERRAM

ANTIQUES OF THE AIR

MICHAEL F JERRAM

09

NEW ENGLISH LIBRARY
TIMES MIRROR

First published in Great Britain by New
English Library, Barnard's Inn, Holborn,
London EC1N 2JR in 1980

Printed in Hong Kong
by South China Printing Co

Produced by
Basinghall Books Limited
59 Cambridge Road
Kings Heath, Birmingham

Designed by Laurence Bradbury

ISBN: 0-450-0-4813-6

CONTENTS

I:PIONEERS

The last Sunday in September is a special day for the vintage aeroplane enthusiast in England, for it is the one day of each year when he may see the Shuttleworth Collection's Edwardian flying machines take to the air. They make an astonishing if incongruous sight, these relics of aviation's infancy, so aptly described by Rudyard Kipling as 'the opening verse of the opening page of the chapter of endless possibilities'.

That any of those faltering 'opening verses' should have survived at all is remarkable, because successful flying machines were never numerous in those early days. Even by 1910 more aeroplanes failed than flew, and those that did fly were marginal craft. Those early pioneers had no design manuals to guide them, no tried and tested constructional techniques on which to depend, and all laboured under a common lack of suitable powerplants. Early aero-engines produced little power for their tremendous weight. They were weak and gravity was strong, so that the aeroplanes were held only just above stalling speed. If the motor stopped (as they did, frequently) the aeroplane stopped soon after and because their airframes were light and lacked inertia it was necessary to put the machine into a steep glide so that the pull of gravity acted directly along its line of flight. If not, a crash was inevitable, as witness this popular little ditty:

> *He died in an hour and a quarter*
> *And this is the reason he died;*
> *He'd forgotten the fact that 'iota'*
> *Was the minimum angle of glide.*

Edwardian designers and aviators were thus students of the trial-and-error school, with sometimes rather more error than trial. Long after the Wright Brothers had

Previous page: The Caudron GIII, which first flew in May 1914, was used during World War I initially on reconnaissance and artillery spotting and later as a trainer. The one pictured is a replica owned by the Jean Salis Collection and built by its founder; it has made several Channel crossings.

successfully demonstrated the possibilities of powered flight – and been called bluffers by sceptical Europeans – would-be fliers were still persisting with long-lost causes such as ornithopters, and for several decades controversy raged over whether the biplane or monoplane configuration was best. The biplane, typified by the Wrights' *Flyer*, was an attractive arrangement, offering a strong and rigid braced-box structure, but nature had few parallels. Birds, which were (and are) the best fliers of all, were monoplanes, but monoplane structures with adequate strength but minimal weight were difficult to build, and many early monoplanes, notably the beautiful Levavasseur Antoinettes, had unenviable records of catastrophic in-flight failures.

Surviving pioneer aircraft in airworthy condition are therefore few and may safely be counted on the fingers of a hand. But their numbers have been boosted by a thriving interest in replica craft, fired perhaps by the film *Those Magnificent Men in Their Flying Machines* for which the technical adviser Air Commodore Allen Wheeler commissioned whole production lines of Edwardian aeroplanes. Such was the enthusiasm for this project that many manufacturers whom he asked to build the aeroplanes had to reject the job for fear that their best design and engineering staff would abandon multi-million-pound government contracts for a chance to work on the old timers. And who could blame them?

There is a schism among old aeroplane enthusiasts on the subject of replicas. Diehard purists insist that modern materials, constructional techniques and engines 'do not an antique make'. Perhaps not, but they do give successive generations a chance to enjoy Kipling's 'opening verse' in its proper element, the air, which as we shall discover, is no greater respecter of man's cleverness now than it was 70 years ago.

The Manning-Flanders was a rather obscure derivative of the Blériot monoplane. This replica was built by Doug Bianchi at Booker airfield for use in a film.

AVRO TRIPLANE

Alliot Verdon Roe's earliest attempts at aviation can scarcely have been encouraging. As a young man working at sea he became fascinated by the flight of birds, and on returning to his parents' home in Manchester he began experimenting with paper gliders which he launched from an upper window of the house. Next door was a lunatic asylum, and before long one of the unfortunate inmates was heard to observe that he feared there was another madman next door. Later, when Roe was flying an early triplane from Lea Marshes in Essex a young woman wrote to him begging to be allowed to try his machine. She was bent on suicide, she confided, but had failed to bring about her death. Mr Roe's flying machine was surely the perfect instrument of her demise?

Despite this lack of encouragement Roe made the first powered flight by an Englishman from Brooklands race track on 8 June 1908, though his achievement was never officially recognised, and went on to develop a series of increasingly successful triplane designs culminating in his 1910 Roe Triplane IV. It was with such a machine that the dastardly Sir Percy Ware-Armitage (played with great elan by comedian Terry Thomas) tried to cheat his fellow rivals in *Those Magnificent Men in Their Flying Machines* and got his come-uppance when he landed atop a speeding train and watched a narrow tunnel neatly remove its wings.

The film-makers chose the Avro because Roe, unlike so many of his contemporaries who were graduates of the Heath Robinson school of engineering, had been a competent professional engineer. They believed that the structure of his Triplane would need little modification to meet modern airworthiness standards. They were right. Roe had meticulously plotted stress paths and devised a fail-safe structure in which no single bracing wire carried the entire load. While piano wire bracing was less reliable than cables (because cables frayed and could thus be spotted during inspections, whereas piano wire failed without warning), at least a sudden twang would not cause a complete structural collapse.

Roe loved wire. His Triplane seemingly had miles of it, so that it reverberates like some kind

of flying harp. The original had a 35hp Green engine, which was just barely capable of overcoming the tremendous drag of the airframe. The *Magnificent Men* replica, now part of the Shuttleworth Trust Collection, has a 90hp Cirrus which is still not over-generous. The replica retains Roe's sophisticated wing-warping for lateral control. The centre and upper wings are hinged at the rear spars so that warping does not actually bend the spars; other wing warping controls invariably depended on the flexibility of wood for their effectiveness and resulted in heavy control forces and poor response. The Avro, in contrast, had moderately light controls for its day, though they are still ponderous by modern standards, and the control wheel has no stops in its lateral movement so that you can go on winding in wing warp until a loud *twang* tells you that you have gone too far. . . .

Roe himself was a frequent victim of the poor lateral control inherent in early aeroplanes. 'It was while making one of these flights' (from Wembley Park in 1909), he recalled, 'that I came to grief. In spite of warping the wing hard over to

The Shuttleworth replica of the 1910 Roe Triplane IV built for the film *Those Magnificent Men in Their Flying Machines.*

counteract the tilt, the machine fell over on its side and crashed. The cause of the accident was the failure to use the rudder for increasing the speed of the falling wingtip. Up to this experience I had failed to appreciate the true worth of the rudder for this special purpose.' So did many other pioneers – and some modern pilots – who tried to raise a wing with aileron at low airspeed and succeeded only in stalling the offending surface and making matters considerably worse.

Pilots who have flown the Shuttleworth Avro report that even a mild 20-degree wing drop seems disastrous because the aeroplane remains intent on turning turtle despite strenuous efforts to right it. There is hardly any interaction between wing-warping and rudder and the open-framework triangular fuselage gives no 'keel' area to aid directional stability. This, remember, was one of the better Edwardian aeroplanes.

The open-frame rear fuselage structure also has a disconcerting habit of flexing alarmingly, adding to the feeling of insecurity which the exposed pilot's position (for there is no cockpit as such) induces in those not used to being naked to the elements from the waist up. The waft of warm air from the engine is at least a comfort, and a useful guide to balanced flight. Warm air (and the inevitable spray of oil) means all is well; a chill draught means that the aeroplane is side-slipping and demands immediate attention.

Roe's original Triplane IV was used as a training aeroplane at Brooklands for a year, during which time it allegedly fell out of the sky on a number of occasions, and in the manner of such things, usually when passing over the sewage farm just outside the perimeter of the racing track. After one year it was scrapped, though whether from damage or accumulated odour is not on record. There are no sewage farms near the Shuttleworth Trust's airfield.

BLACKBURN MONOPLANE

'I got into a terrific wobble, came down in a nose dive from the great height of two feet and crashed the machine, landing on my head in the sand', recalled Robert Blackburn of his very first attempt at aviating. 'However,' he added laconically, 'this did not dim my faith in aeroplanes.'

Blackburn was working in France in 1908 when Wilbur Wright took his *Flyer* to Le Mans and so astonished European observers with his prowess that one declared in exasperation: 'We are beaten! We just don't exist!' On his return to England Blackburn started building his first aeroplane, a well-engineered monoplane powered by a 35hp Green water-cooled engine in which the pilot sat in a sliding wicker chair in an under-slung cage so that he could move back and forth to alter the aeroplane's centre of gravity. He also devised a clever 'all-in-one' control system whereby a motorcar's steering wheel was turned to operate the rudder, moved up and down for the elevator, and from side to side to warp the wings. He even planned an auto-stabiliser worked by compressed air to maintain level flight automatically, though it was never fitted.

It was on this machine that Blackburn did his head-in-the-sand act at Marske-by-Sea in Yorkshire in April 1909. Bentfield 'Benny' Hucks, later to become a popular figure as one of the pioneer aerobatics pilots, met Blackburn at the 1910 Blackpool Flying Carnival where he was working for Claude Grahame-White and joined his enterprise as test pilot, though at the time Hucks had no pilot's certificate and effectively taught himself to fly while testing a succession

The Shuttleworth Blackburn is the oldest British aeroplane still flying.

of Blackburn's monoplanes.

A 50hp Gnome rotary-engined Blackburn Monoplane was flown by Hucks in the 1911 *Daily Mail* Circuit of Britain air race which started and finished at Brooklands and took in Hendon, Harrogate, Newcastle, Edinburgh, Stirling, Paisley, Carlisle, Manchester, Bristol, Exeter, Salisbury and Brighten en route. Prizes totalled £10,000 and about 30,000 spectators watched the start in foul weather on 22 July. Poor Hucks got no further than Luton, when an engine failure forced him down and the Blackburn was too badly damaged to carry on. This same machine was later used to make the first practical demonstration of ground-to-air radiotelephony.

Blackburn's seventh Monoplane was a specially commissioned machine (perhaps the first ever custom-built aeroplane) for a Mr Cyril Foggin, who learned to fly with the Blackburn School at Hendon and was a well-known sporting flier before World War I. This 1912 Blackburn Single-Seat Monoplane still exists and is the oldest original British machine still flying. The enormous responsibility of caring for such a treasure rests with the Shuttleworth Trust, which acquired the Blackburn in 1938. After several public exhibitions in the hands of Cyril Foggins during 1913 the Blackburn was bought by another Hendon graduate, one Francis Glew, who crashed it the following year and stored the remains on his farm at Wittering, Lincolnshire. It remained there for a quarter-century, partly covered by a haystack but complete even to spare parts for its 50hp Gnome rotary engine. Of such lucky finds is the very stuff of antique aviation made.

The 1912 Monoplane was more compact and lighter than its predecessors and looks remarkably modern alongside its Avro Triplane and Bristol Boxkite stablemates. The triangular-section fuselage is fully covered and the oil-slinging Gnome is handsomely clothed in a streamlined aluminium half-cowling. Gone is Blackburn's patent triple steering column, replaced by conventional pedals for the rudder with a wheel and column for roll and pitch control, still reminiscent of a sportscar steering wheel. The column moves in an unfamiliar manner, straight downwards until it almost touches the pilot's thighs for 'up' elevator and upwards until it almost obscures his forward vision for 'down'. Very confusing. Equally alarming is the way in which a solid-looking fuselage crossmember blocks entrance to the cockpit, until you learn that it hinges upwards and then clips back to form a safety bar.

Showing a neater and cleaner appearance than most of its contemporaries, the original

1912 Blackburn Monoplane restored to flying condition by the Shuttleworth Trust.

The Blackburn's cockpit is undemanding, for there is just a solitary instrument, an engine revolutions counter for the Gnome. And what is this, on the left, which looks like an old brass Victorian light switch? Why, it is a Victorian light switch, of course, pressed into service as a magneto switch, while another ignition cut-out button is mounted on the control wheel to 'blip' the engine with the characteristic *brrp-brrrp-brrrp* of a rotary powerplant. Shuttleworth pilots claim that it occasionally zaps them with little electric shocks.

Let us watch the Blackburn fly. The air, of course, is calm. The pilot, suitably clad in warm oilproof clothing befitting his spartan accommodation, mounts the machine (Edwardian pilots always 'mounted' their machines, like horse-riders). One of the ground crew produces a huge brass syringe (also used for horses . . .) and begins to minister to the Gnome, injecting neat petrol into each of the seven cylinders, while the pilot tends to the three levers which control (but only just) its running — a throttle of sorts which 'works in theory only', an air lever and a fine adjustment lever, which together demand the dexterity of a Wurlitzer organist.

Contact! On goes the brass light switch; round goes the propeller; *clonk-clonk-clonk* goes the Gnome, puffing out a cloud of blue-grey castor-oil smoke, then settling down to a merry sewing-machine hum. Paradoxically the early rotary engines, whose cylinders spin with the propeller around a fixed hollow crankshaft, do not rattle and vibrate as many suppose they do; properly adjusted they run as smoothly as turbines.

Taxiing demands three pairs of hands — one pair in the cockpit and another at each wingtip, because these lightweight brakeless aeroplanes have poor directional control on the ground and weathercock into the slightest puff of wind. The Blackburn has been making full flights (as opposed to straight up-down hops) only since 1973. Here is how the late Neil Williams remembered his first fraught circuit in the machine in *Pilot* magazine:

'Straight and true she rolled, accelerating gently, but this time hopefully she would not be made to stop . . . I pressed gently on the wheel and she was off cleanly . . . I was two-thirds down the field at about 30 feet. Now was the time to stop — or never. The machine was willing — now we were committed, but as I left the field behind me she was starting to sink; with mounting alarm I flew as carefully as I knew how, coaxing her, giving a little, taking a little. Down, down, now we were only ten feet over the standing corn,

the engine still pulling with all of its tiny heart. And slowly, very slowly, again we started to climb . . . and I concentrated on gaining height before trying a turn back to the field. I knew that everyone on the field was deeply concerned [*and so was Neil, fearing that if he damaged this unique and priceless gem he might have to flee the country, so terrible would be the wrath of the Shuttleworth Trust's manager David Ogilvy*], but I placed my trust in that sturdy little engine and kept climbing.'

At length he succeeded in persuading the Blackburn to climb to 700 feet and made a turn back to the airfield, where he arrived soaked in castor oil and bathed in relief. One wonders how men like Blackburn and Hucks ever taught themselves to fly in such machines. Courageous they were, in spirit and in pocket; one pioneer claimed his bills to rectify the inevitable spate of 'upsets' set him back £1500 a month. Small wonder that few of the aeroplanes survived.

BLERIOT XI MONOPLANE

Alessandro Anzani had a reputation for using the foulest language. Those familiar with the aero-engines which the Italian ex-motorcycle racer and manufacturer built will understand why: Anzani engines would have made a saint swear. They were cantankerous and recalcitrant in the extreme, forever overheating, and losing power, of which they had precious little to lose to begin with.

Yet it was behind such a device that the first and perhaps the most famous aeroplane voyage was made. Not since 1066 had the arrival of a Frenchman on British soil been of such epoch-making significance as was Louis Blériot's landfall at Dover after his pioneering flight across the English Channel on 25 July 1909. 'Britain is no longer an island!' the press baron Lord Northcliffe warned darkly, while congratulating the Frenchman on winning the £1000 prize put up by his newspaper. Everyone was inspired by this triumph, except perhaps the dour customs official who insisted on examining M Blériot's 'vessel' — by then flopped like an exhausted seagull near Dover Castle — for signs of contraband or contagious disease. The 21-mile crossing was no small achievement. The 37-minute duration of the flight was almost certainly the longest period for which an Anzani engine had

Possibly the world's most well-known aircraft is the Blériot XI Monoplane. The one pictured is part-original and part-reproduction of the first aeroplane to cross the English Channel and is owned by the Salis Collection.

A closer view of the Salis Blériot, which itself has been flown twice across the English Channel.

This one of the many Blériot replicas is owned by the de Havilland Mosquito Museum in England.

until then run uninterrupted, but even so Blériot barely made it. Part way across the motor began overheating and only a fortuitous rainshower cooled its cylinders and prevented a ditching – a fate which had twice befallen Blériot's close rival, Hubert Latham.

Blériot was a shrewd businessman. He had made his fortune manufacturing acetylene lamps for motorcars, and blew nearly all of it dabbling with flying machines. He tried every conceivable configuration before settling on the monoplane layout which today remains the most familiar form for aeroplanes – wings at the front, tail at the rear. For him the Channel attempt was an opportunity to publicise his machines, and it worked. Within two days of the flight orders for more than 100 machines flooded in and soon Blériot Monoplanes were in widespread use at training schools and in military service throughout the world.

Fittingly for such a famous machine, a number of Blériots are still flying. The Shuttleworth Trust in England has one which is the oldest aeroplane in the collection and probably the oldest aeroplane flying anywhere in the world, though contrary to popular myth it is not Blériot's original Channel-crosser. That machine, having been given leave to proceed by the Dover customs man, actually never flew again, and hangs today in the Conservatoire des Arts et Métiers in Paris.

Jean Salis, who keeps a fine collection of vintage aircraft at La Ferté Alais to the southwest of Paris has a part-original Blériot XI which his father Jean-Baptiste discovered as a wreck and twice flew across the English Channel, once in 1954 and again in 1959 to commemorate the 50th anniversary of Blériot's flight. And Cole Palen, founder of the Old Rhinebeck Collection in New York State, has two flying Blériots – a 1909 model discovered in a junkyard, and a 1911 model built by the American Aeroplane Supply Company of Long Island which was stored in a barn from 1915 until 1963, when it was slightly damaged in a fire; it has since been restored.

There might yet be other Blériots sleeping quietly in lofts and barns, waiting to be rediscovered. Who knows? The Shuttleworth's 1909 aeroplane flew for three years with the Blériot School at Hendon before it was damaged in a crash and sold to a scrap merchant, who stored it under the railway arches at Blackfriars until the Collection's first benefactor, A E Grimmer, bought it and made repairs before teaching himself to fly. 'As I made my first attempt to leave the ground,' he wrote of his trials at Postern

Two views of the original
1909 Blériot XI restored by
the Shuttleworth Trust.
It is probably the oldest
aeroplane in the world still
regularly flying.

The Shuttleworth Blériot
XI in flight.

Piece, Bedfordshire, on Easter Monday 1913, 'an old chap of about 90 wandered across the fairway. Only by jumping out of my seat and hanging on to the side of the machine did I manage to avoid hitting him. The second attempt might well have proved more successful than the first. This time "Mad Jack", a local character, deliberately ran out into my path, leaping high and opening his umbrella, to land in imitation of a parachute jumper . . . I knew Jack for a pretty active fellow, and I also knew how short the field was, so I ignored Jack's presence, and, more by reason of a dip in the ground than as a result of engine power, I found myself airborne.'

Mr Grimmer continued to fly his Blériot until war broke out and recalled that the Irish linen which he had purchased to re-cover it provided enough left-over material for summer dresses for his sisters and new curtains for the house. By one of those rare serendipitous chances he attended a meeting in Bedford in 1935 about the opening of a proposed Bedford Municipal Airport and there met Richard Shuttleworth, founder of the splendid collection of aeroplanes and motorcars which bears his name. Would Mr Shuttleworth like a 1909 Blériot Monoplane and a 1910 Deperdussin, he wondered? The two machines were collected a few days later. Parts of the Blériot were missing, but were discovered on a rubbish heap with an elder tree growing through them. Restoration took the best part of two years. Since then the two machines have remained at Old Warden Aerodrome as the keystones of the Shuttleworth Collection.

On first sight the most striking thing about the Blériot is its size; the aeroplane is quite tiny, spanning just 25 feet. The broad wings are heavily cambered and supported by what looks like a skeletal circus 'big top' of bracing wires fanning out from kingposts. Blériot employed wing warping for lateral control, taking advantage of the natural flexure of the light structure, though he had earlier experimented with and abandoned ailerons. The fuselage is an open lattice-work frame with canvas snap-on covers extending to just aft of the pilot's wickerwork seat. The ordinary bicycle wheels which Blériot employed are free-castoring and sprung on rubber bungee cord. They make ground handling interesting and even getting aboard difficult, for as you take hold of the machine to haul yourself up, it sidles away from you as if it would rather you left it alone.

In its day the Blériot Monoplane was a modern machine which first featured the logical system of control adopted by virtually every aeroplane since. The control stick is universally jointed to a patented bell-shaped housing on the cockpit floor and controls wing warping and elevator in the natural sense (stick left, left wing down; stick back, nose up and so forth), while a pair of pedals directs the rudder.

The engine is one of Signor Anzani's masterpieces, a three-cylinder motor whose cylinder barrels are arranged in a fan shape (and strangely, on the Shuttleworth aircraft at least, the angle between each barrel and the next is different) which is supposed to produce about 25hp. Lubrication is by a total-loss castor-oil system pressurised by a rubber bulb in the cockpit. Total loss is a misnomer, for the oil is not so much lost as sprayed in a fine vapourised haze all over the unfortunate pilot, who likely also suffers from blurred vision from the engine's vibration.

'Ready when you are.' 'Contact.' A ground crewman swings the polished wood scimitar of a propeller and (sometimes) away goes the Anzani, *pok-pok-pok-pok-tapoketa-pok-pok-pok-pok-pok*, like a mechanical hen. The sweet scent of castor oil mixes with the smell of new-mown grass as the ground handlers take hold of a wingtip each to guide this treasure to the take-off point. If the wind is more than five knots the Blériot does not fly, nor does it take off other than directly into the breeze, for it has poor directional control and the Anzani is capable of lifting it at best maybe 50 feet, so flights take the form of long straight-line hops.

The Blériot's elevators consist of hinged outboard panels of the tailplane, and the aeroplanes were always noted for their sensitivity in pitch. A moment's inattention and the Blériot will rear up and the airspeed (at best 25–35mph) begins to bleed off quickly. Early Anzani-engined Blériots were tail heavy which probably accounted for this phenomenon; later models had heavier Gnome rotary engines, and were in all respects much better machines whose lively performance was exploited by early aerobatics fliers.

Such a flier was Adolphe Pégoud, a protégé of Blériot's, who prepared himself for this *ballet aerienne* by reading his daily newspaper while suspended upside down in a chair. When Pégoud came to England with his specially modified Blériot XI and astonished a sceptical crowd at Brooklands with loops, sideslips and 'somersaults' (what we now call a roll) the British aviator and promoter Claude Grahame-White threw a celebratory upside-down dinner at which all tables were inverted, the courses were served in reverse order, and the music hall

comedian Charles Coburn sang *Two Lovely Black Eyes* while standing on his head.

Pégoud made flying a Blériot look easy. By contemporary standards it *was* an easy machine to handle, indeed Louis himself had barely five hours of piloting experience when he crossed the Channel, and promised his wife that he would never fly again if he won the prize. Madame Blériot was not surprised when he broke his word.

BRISTOL BOXKITE

Ever seen a galleon fly? The next best thing is the sight of a Bristol Boxkite airborne. As its name suggests the Boxkite is a mixture of kite and aeroplane which was a direct descendant of the successful French machines built by the brotherly duo, Farman and Voisin, and was the first commercially produced British aeroplane. Sir George White, millionaire owner of the Bristol Tramways Company, became interested in aerial transport and set up the British & Colonial Aeroplane Company (later to become the Bristol Aeroplane Company) to produce Henri Farman's designs under licence. Taking a proven design rather than starting afresh proved sound commercial policy and after its debut at the Third International Aero Exhibition at Olympia in 1911 the Boxkite was produced at the then-unheard-of rate of two each week; it was selected by the armies of Britain and Russia and widely exported throughout the British Empire, priced at about £1000.

Not one of the 133 Boxkites built survives in airworthy condition, but a replica constructed for *Those Magnificent Men in Their Flying Machines* wafts grandly into the air once a year with the Shuttleworth Trust. It is a bizarre device, a tangled forest of struts and wires in seemingly

The monstrous Bristol Boxkite is still flown occasionally but only in halcyon weather.

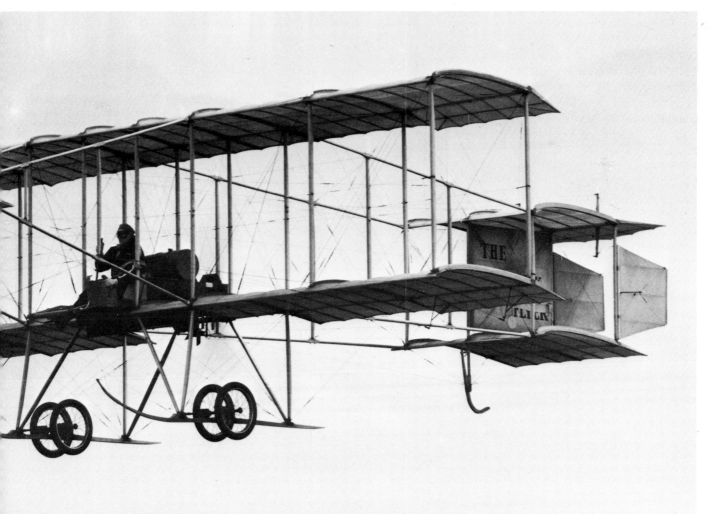

Awaiting their call to take
to the air at Old Warden
are the Shuttleworth
Trust's Bristol Boxkite and
the Blériot and Blackburn
Monoplanes.

Bristol Boxkite 1910 replica in flight at Old Warden.

in Boxkites back in 1910 army observers were quick to reply 'layer after layer of warm clothing'.

Curiously, the Boxkite's wings are fabric-covered on one side only, the spars and ribs simply being faired over with narrow strips of material which give the surfaces a half-starved appearance. Disconcerting too is the way in which the ailerons all droop on the ground, hanging limply on slack control wires. Once moving, the slipstream raises the surfaces to their normal position, though they work only in the 'down' sense, the opposite aileron remaining neutral. Control is effected by a conventional stick of enormous proportions whose handgrip is almost at eye level, and since the control cables are attached near the top considerable effort is needed in stirring the stick to get enough leverage.

The original Boxkites were mostly powered by 50hp Gnome rotary engines. The combination of gyroscopic forces from the heavy spinning motor and the poor aileron response made it all but impossible to make left turns — there was simply insufficient aileron power to oppose the machine's desire to turn right. For the replica Miles substituted a modern 65hp Rolls-Royce Continental engine, reasonably supposing that some throttle-limiting might be necessary to contain the additional power. Quite the opposite proved to be true. On 65hp the Boxkite barely flew at all and was hard pressed to maintain altitude, while the engine overheated and was plagued with carburetter ice, further reducing its output.

The reason was simple: the old rotary engines swung large-diameter propellers and thus produced more thrust than modern powerplants, and since the entire engine rotated about its crankshaft cooling was not a problem. Replacing the 65hp engine with a 90hp engine made the Boxkite more manageable, but even so the motor was unable to produce as much thrust as the 50hp Gnome, which ran at half the speed.

Flying the Boxkite is reportedly like riding a soft blancmange through a Force Nine gale. Since the opportunity to do either has never come my way I offer the late Neil Williams's opinion that the Boxkite 'is the very devil to fly'. He claimed that the machine would maintain level flight at just one speed — precisely 31mph. One might therefore be surprised to learn that during the making of *Those Magnificent Men* film flier Derek Piggot actually embarked on a few leisurely cross-country flights in the Boxkite . . . very leisurely. From Skegness to Booker in Buckinghamshire, a distance of 121 miles, took

loose formation which simply does not look as if it will ever fly. It does, but barely, and not too well, though an optimistic publicity puff put out by the builders in 1910 assured potential owners that its control system was 'simplicity itself and can be mastered in a few minutes (with) so little physical effort that a child can manoeuvre one of these machines in flight'.

I do not suppose a child ever actually tried it, but the Boxkite *was* much used as a training machine with the Bristol flying schools at Larkhill and Brooklands. Robert Smith-Barry, the father of the Gosport training system, was one pilot who gained his wings on it.

The Shuttleworth replica was built by the Miles Aircraft Company at Shoreham, Sussex, who found that the design's structural stressing compared not unfavourably with modern practice. Not so the Boxkite's configuration, which looks as if it might have been fashioned as an exercise in colossal drag. There is no fuselage as such, nor any cockpit. The pilot and passenger (for which position there are few volunteers) sit at the wing's leading edge ahead of the engine in vertigo-inducing insecurity, though one gets an unrivalled view of the slowly passing countryside. Not surprisingly, when asked what equipment might be needed for aerial reconnaissance him three hours and 35 minutes, averaging a very respectable (for Boxkites) 33.8mph and considerably slowing traffic on the M1 motorway when he overflew it. But a short 38-mile hop from Booker to RAF Henlow took almost two hours at a dismal ground speed of 20mph. A good athlete could almost do as well; a racing cyclist would have left him far behind.

I need hardly mention therefore that the Shuttleworth Boxkite does not fly in any but the merest zephyr of wind, the like of which would scarcely support its namesake. But when it does, oh, what a sight – stately as a sailing ship, and with more singing wires than a grand piano.

CURTISS PUSHER

Hammondsport in western New York State is noted in two respects – for the excellent wines produced by the local vineyards, and as the birthplace of one of America's foremost aviation pioneers, Glenn Hammond Curtiss.

Like his contemporaries, the Wright Brothers, Curtiss was in business as a bicycle maker and repairer, and was noted for the excellent engines which he developed for motorcycles, one of

which earned him the title of 'World's Fastest Human Being' on 24 January 1907 when he rode at the then-astonishing speed of 137mph at Ormond Beach, Florida.

Curtiss's engines had high power/weight ratios, a rare and much sought-after commodity among early aviators, and it was perhaps inevitable that he should have been drawn towards aviation – albeit reluctantly at first – as a member of Alexander Graham Bell's Aerial Experiment Association.

Appropriately, it was on 4 July 1908 that

Two views of the Curtiss Pusher replica regularly flown by Dale Crites, who donated a previously owned original Pusher to the Curtiss Museum in the US.

Curtiss came to prominence as a flier. On that day he flew his *June Bug* biplane 5090 feet in one minute 42.2 seconds to win the *Scientific American* Trophy for the first publicly witnessed flight of over one kilometre in the United States of America. The *June Bug* looked not unlike the Wright's *Flyer* in configuration, having a single forward elevator and a biplane tail enclosing the rudder, but Curtiss installed a 40hp V-8 engine of his own design to drive its single pusher propeller and fitted a tricycle undercarriage, the first such to be used successfully on an aeroplane. Lateral control was provided by movable wingtips, which led to a protracted and bitter legal action by the Wrights, who claimed that Curtiss had infringed their wing-warping patents. The matter was not settled for many years, when the Curtiss-

The Curtiss Pusher pictured as the US Navy's first aircraft.

Dale Crites has time to acknowledge the appreciation of spectators as he flies past in his Curtiss Pusher replica.

Wright Corporation was founded and long after the principal protagonists had left the scene.

The Independence Day flight was a heady moment for the young motorcycle racer, even though his speed through the air (39mph) was little more than a quarter what he had already achieved on land. 'When I gave the word to let go of the *June Bug*,' he recalled, 'she skimmed along over the old racetrack for perhaps two hundred feet and then rose gracefully in the air. The crowd set up a cheer, as I was told later, for I could hear nothing but the roar of the motor and I saw nothing except the course and the flag marking the distance of one kilometre. The flag was quickly reached and passed and I still kept the aeroplane up, flying as far as the open fields would permit, and finally coming down safely in

a meadow fully a mile from the starting place. I might have gone a good deal farther as the motor was working perfectly and I had the machine under perfect control, but to have prolonged the flight would have meant a turn in the air.'

A turn in the air was to be avoided at all costs in those days, for the aeroplane's ailerons were there to correct rather than initiate roll movements. Stability rather than controllability was the aim.

For the *Grand Semaine d'Aviation* at Rheims in August 1909 Glenn Curtiss produced an improved aircraft called the *Golden Flyer* (because of the yellow-gold colour of its varnished silk covering) which he built to the order of the Aeronautical Society of New York. The *Golden Flyer* had wings of reduced area, of rectangular shape and with no dihedral. 'Winglet' ailerons were mounted at the midpoints of the interplane struts to avoid further claims from the Wrights, whose patent applied to roll controls which were an integral part of the wing, and a 60hp V-8 Curtiss engine was installed. On 28 August 1909 Curtiss flew this machine to victory in the Gordon Bennett Cup, averaging 43.35mph for the 20-kilometre course, and was briefly the fastest man on land and in the air.

From the basic *Golden Flyer* design came a host of Curtiss pusher biplanes offered with a variety of engines from 26 to 90hp. At the suggestion of the great barnstormer and stunt pilot Lincoln Beachey, and very much against his own judgement, Curtiss experimentally abandoned the forward elevator and thus created the archetypal 'Headless' Curtiss, a design which has since been much copied. Curtiss himself built a replica for nostalgia's sake after World War I; it is displayed at the National Air & Space Museum in Washington, DC, and a *June Bug* replica is on show at the Glenn H Curtiss Museum of Local History in Hammondsport.

A number of Curtiss Pusher replicas are flying in the United States, and one in Europe with Jean Salis at La Ferté Alais (*see Chapter 5*). One of the best is owned by American antique aircraft enthusiast Dale Crites, who once had a genuine Pusher which he donated to the Curtiss Museum after a crash. Crites is a brave man. He chose not to go the easy route in his replica by installing a reliable modern powerplant, but instead sought out a genuine 90hp Curtiss OX-5 V-8 liquid-cooled engine. The adjective 'brave' is used to describe Crites because the OX-5 is not the most dependable of motors and is widely known as 'a failure looking for somewhere to happen' among veteran American pilots. It weighs 377 pounds, overheats at the least provocation and spews water like a sieve. Old-timers who learned to fly in OX-5-powered aeroplanes formed their own club (either for celebration of commiseration, I know not which).

Crites's Pusher also features the bamboo pole fuselage booms of the original and – a nice touch this – a pair of huge horse-blanket safety pins to attach the forward surface of the tailplane to the outriggers. Not quite string and chewing gum, but almost. . . .

Despite its apparent crudeness, the Curtiss Pusher had an advanced control system. A steering wheel mounted on a control column provided pitch and yaw commands, while the ailerons were operated by a yoke which fitted around the pilot's shoulders so that the aeroplane's 'balance' could be maintained by swaying the body in the appropriate direction. It took a motorcyclist to think of that. On two-seat Pushers the control wheel could be swung over to enable either occupant to fly. An ignition advance lever was fitted for the pilot's left hand and there were three foot controls: one allowing an extra charge of oil to be pumped to the engine; another to shut off the ignition and, if pushed to its limit, to brake the front wheel; and a third for throttle control. Wheel brakes were an innovation indeed, and the shoulder yolk worked well enough except that a turn of the head to look behind could result in an involuntary wing drop unless care was taken.

The Curtiss's manoeuvrability made it popular with early airshow performers. Lincoln Beachey, who used a Pusher to perform the first loop in the United States and to set a world altitude record of 11,642ft on 20 August 1911, barnstormed with the Curtiss Exhibition Fliers and is said to have earned as much as $4000 a week stunting and giving car-versus-aeroplane exhibitions with great racing drivers such as Barney Oldfield and Eddie Rickenbacker. Beachey later flew a Curtiss-inspired Pusher biplane called *Little Looper* which had an 80hp Gnome rotary engine and could

perform advanced aerobatics including inside and outside loops, triple-reverses (consecutive inside-outside-inside loops), rolls, sustained inverted flight, and even gain altitude while looping, something which no other contemporary aircraft could do.

Frank Tallman, the late movie flier and stunt pilot, flew Curtiss Pusher replicas for several films and noted in his book, *Flying the Old Planes*, that the aircraft had 'supersensitive' controls, a rare tribute for a machine from an era when control response was usually slow and ponderous and occasionally non-existent. 'The tiniest movement of the wheel caused a sudden pitch-up or nose-down,' he wrote, 'and only the landing saved a roller coaster ride that would make Coney Island pale by comparison.'

The Pusher won permanent fame by making the first ship take-off from USS *Birmingham* in November 1910 and the first ship landing on the *Prnnsylvania* in January 1911 as these pictures record.

PIONEERS: A REVIEW

The Shuttleworth Collection's precious original 1910 Deperdussin comes in to a safe landing at Old Warden after one of its regular airshow flying displays. Armand Deperdussin, founder of the SPAD of World War I fame, was one of the chief originators of monocoque construction.

The Manning-Flanders was a rather obscure derivative of the Blériot Monoplane. This replica was built by Doug Bianchi at Booker airfield for use in a film.

Must have "SHELL at all costs!

TRIUMPHS OF THE AIR

Mr. L. I. PAULHAN writes:

"I used "SHELL" on my flight from London to Manchester, and from start to finish the Gnome Engine ran splendidly, which is a fine tribute to the quality and uniformity of "SHELL" Motor Spirit.

Right: With motoring settling down into routine by the second decade of the century, the advent of the practical flying machine brought a whole new dimension to advertising, typified by these two Shell advertisements.

Far right: This replica of a 1910 Hanriot Monoplane was built in 1974 for the Old Rhinebeck Collection, where it is still flown regularly. A peculiarity which modern pilots must find needs deep concentration is that it has two control columns, one for elevators and the other for wing warping.

The Salis Collection's Caudron G-III during one of its Channel flights.

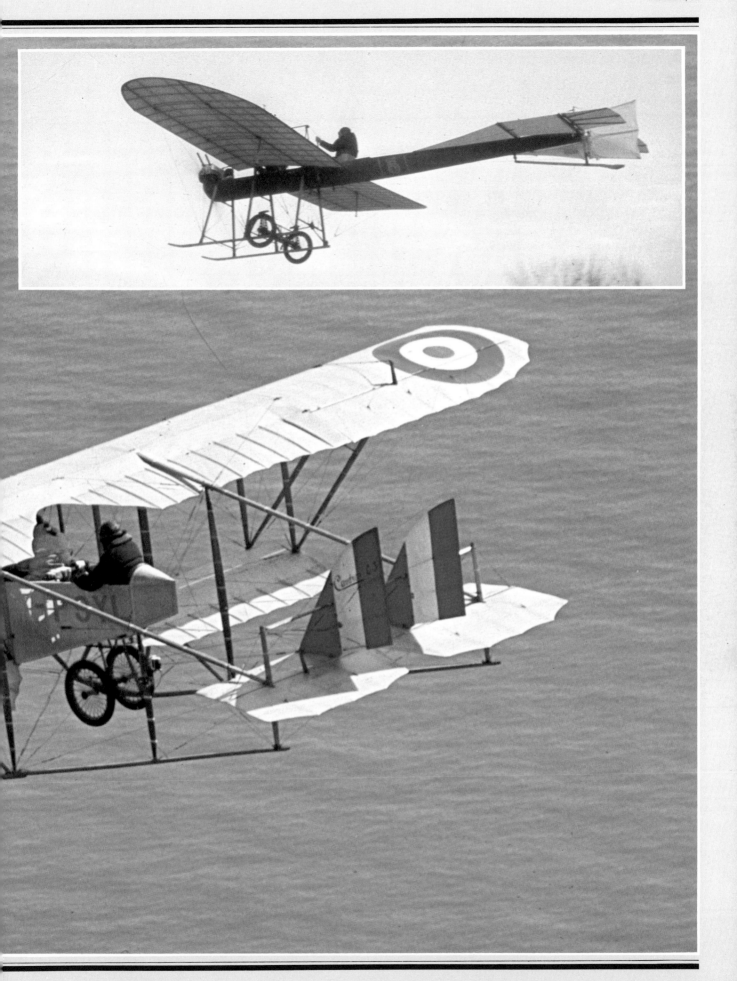

Although the Fokker E III Eindecker was a 1915 development, it still found the extensive wire wing bracing of the earlier monoplanes essential. This replica was built by Doug Bianchi for the film *Crooks and Coronets* and is owned and still flown by his son Tony.

Giuseppe Bellanca, who later became an expert in aerofoil design, taught himself to fly on his first monoplane, built in 1912. This replica pictured at Old Rhinebeck, still flies and is still privately owned; its owner recently married and has installed a second seat for his wife.

2:GREAT WAR

Nothing concentrates the inventive mind like a war. Thus, between the years 1914 and 1919 – barely a moment in man's agonising centuries-long quest for flight – aeroplanes developed from fragile curiosities into powerful weapons, from Boxkites to multi-engined bombers which for the first time could spread destruction across national boundaries, beyond the muddy, bloody battlefields to the very hearts of nations, just as Lord Northcliffe had predicted when he foresaw an end to Britain's comfortable insularity with Louis Blériot's tentative hop across the English Channel.

Few people saw any military future for the aeroplane on that fateful day at Sarajevo in June 1914, least of all apopleptic old cavalry generals who feared only that the newfangled flying machines might startle their mounts (and rob them of their purpose in reconnaissance and pursuit, which they did). At least one struck a last futile blow for the horse-soldiers; just five weeks into the war a French lieutenant named Gironde, trying to escape the German advance towards the Marne, led one of the last cavalry charges in history against a squadron of German Aviatik observation aircraft and destroyed them on the ground.

For the first few months of the war flying machines were unarmed passive observers, but their role in reconnaissance was quickly recognised, and equally swiftly was realised the need to deny enemy aircraft freedom of the skies. The earliest aerial encounters were comic-opera performances, gentlemanly exchanges

An important Morane-Saulnier World War I type was the AI parasol monoplane, of which more than 1200 were delivered. This MoS. A1 is one of three replicas built by the Salis concern.

of fire by aerial duellists for whom the choice of weapons was left to expediency and limited by the inability of the early aircraft to lift a pilot, observer and machine gun to any worthwhile height.

Left with a choice of carrying men or weapons it was the gunner who was dispensed with, and thus — almost by accident — was the single-seat fighter born, although almost throughout the war such aircraft were still known as scouts, reflecting their primary role in observation rather than aggression. When a young Dutch engineer named Anthony Fokker first perfected a device which permitted a a machine gun to be mounted along the centreline of an aeroplane and fired through its propeller arc (enabling the machine to be aimed directly at its target) the concept of aerial warfare changed and for a few months in the autumn of 1915, Fokker's Eindeckers carved a deadly swathe through the skies of France — a time which became known as the Fokker Scourge.

During five years of conflict the aeroplane as a weapon was honed to a fine edge on the stone of necessity, and produced in enormous quantities — more than 5000 Sopwith Camels; 14,000 SPADs; 1000 Fokker D7s, a type so formidable that the Allies named it specifically in their list of war spoils after the Armistice.

Where are they now? Most have disappeared. There are many World War I aircraft in museums around the world, but flying examples are rare. Not a single airworthy Camel exists, nor an Albatros, and not one original Fokker Triplane of any kind, but interest in Great War machines runs high and there is a thriving business in the construction of replicas.

World War I aircraft lend themselves well to replica-building. Their structures were mostly well-engineered and straightforward in construction, and modern radial or inline powerplants suitably disguised behind fibreglass cowlings make fine substitutes for the oil-throwing rotaries of Pups, Camels and Triplanes or the water-cooled masterpieces that powered the Albatroses, Fokkers and SPADs.

For less than £100 you can buy a set of plans to build a replica of the Red Baron's Dreidecker (more than 60 are flying). Lay them out on your living room floor and dream of playing the 'Hun in the Sun'; or reach for your silk scarf and goggles and browse through *World War One Aeroplanes*, a non-profit-making magazine run by a New York schoolmaster for Great War enthusiasts and would-be Dawn Patrollers. Its classified advertisements contain the most amazing offers and wants: a zero-time 80hp Le Rhone rotary engine; a Zeppelin rudder bar (in case anyone should have the rest of it?); a complete flying Pfalz D.III replica; dummy Spandau machine guns which spit not lead but gas-generated muzzle flashes. Of such stuff are latter-day aces' dreams made.

And in England Leisure Sport Limited, a company which runs a Disney-style theme park not far from London Heathrow Airport, has assembled a veritable flying circus of World War I replicas; there are three Sopwith Camels, a SPAD, Fokkers DR1 and D.7, a Nieuport, a 1½-Strutter and even a funny little de Havilland DH 2 in which the observer sat in a bathtub-like fuselage ahead of his pilot and had to be very careful not to drop ammunition drums when changing them lest the slipstream take them clean through the pusher propeller and flimsy tailbooms. The Leisure Sport collection is not yet completed; more early warbirds are planned, but secrecy prevails. A Handley Page O/400 'bloody paralyser' bomber perhaps? Or one of the Zeppelin-Staacken giants? Nostalgia knows no bounds.

AVRO 504

Which is the world's most successful aeroplane? It depends of course on what you mean by successful, but if longevity of service, ready adaptability to widely varying roles and universal affection are key factors, the Avro 504 has few rivals for the title.

The Avro 504 was designed early in 1913 (in a penny exercise book!) by Alliot Verdon Roe, whose Triplane we examined in Chapter 1. From its earliest test flights at Brooklands the 80hp Gnome-powered biplane showed superlative handling qualities. Its airframe was, like the Triplane's, an engineering masterpiece. 'It looks astonishingly light,' one critic observed. 'No,' said Roe, 'it should rather be said that it is astonishingly strong for its weight.' The 504 was indeed a fine machine, but even so Roe considered himself lucky to win orders for six aircraft, little knowing that by Armistice Day the total would have been raised to 8340 and that

well over 10,000 of his two-seat biplanes would eventually be built worldwide.

At the outbreak of war in 1914 military aeroplanes were in short supply for the purpose of 'transporting a trained observer to obtain information of the enemy positions and actions', a role which the Avro fitted splendidly. Both the War Office and Admiralty placed orders and it fell to Royal Flying Corps Avro 504As and Royal Naval Air Service 504Bs to achieve the double distinction of being the first Allied aircraft shot down in combat and the first to make bombing raids on Germany. The first incident occurred on 22 August 1914 when an Avro flown by a Lieutenant Waterfall from 5 Squadron RFC was dispatched by groundfire; the second on 22 September of that year when four RNAS Avros led by Flight Lieutenant Collett attacked the Zeppelin sheds at Friedrichshafen and severely damaged the local gasworks in the process.

Avros were converted as anti-Zeppelin fighters with a single Lewis gun mounted at the centre section of the upper wing and the forward cock-

Right: This 1918 Avro 504K was retored in 1967 and is maintained in flying condition by Canada's National Aeronautical Collection.

Below: Almost a perfect three-pointer as the Shuttleworth 504K lands.

pit faired over, and one enterprising flight commander actually managed to bomb a Zeppelin, by flying 200 feet above it and releasing his 20-pounders, but the gasbag failed to explode.

But it was as a training aeroplane that the Avro was to excel, thanks initially to its selection by the father of air training methods, Major Robert Smith-Barry, for his Special School of Flying at Gosport in Hampshire. From 1915 until 1933 Avro 504s of various marks formed the vanguard of military training aeroplanes in the Royal Flying Corps and Royal Air Force. Best known were the Avro 504J and 504K on which (among tens of thousands of his subjects) His Royal Highness Prince Albert, later to become King George VI, learned to fly.

The Avro 504K could be powered by 100hp Gnome, 110hp Le Rhone or 130hp Clerget rotary engines which all fitted a common mount. As its name suggests, the Monosoupape had but a single valve in each of its seven cylinders serving both as an air inlet and exhaust valve, the fuel mixture being fed in through a fixed hollow crankshaft.

As with so many contemporary aircraft, the most difficult part of the Avro's handling for a novice lay in mastering the idiosyncrasies of the motor, despite the Pilot's Notes assurance that 'running the engine is simple'. Also, with its narrow-track undercarriage the Avro was a notorious ground-looper, though the characteristic 'toothpick' skid helped to prevent nose-overs.

Who knows how many student pilots sweated and strained through their first flying hours on Avros, cursing the sensitivity of the Mono engine which was unthrottled save for a blip switch and was prone to lose power if the mixture was set too rich and then come on with a sudden burst of energy just when you had her lined up for a power-off forced landing, wafting your way past the field before cutting again because you had closed the fuel lever when she first coughed and spluttered? Hardly surprising that of the 8000 Avros manufactured in wartime, only about 3000 remained on charge in November 1918. The practice, having wrecked your machine, was simply to go to stores and indent for a new one, even though they did cost £870 each, plus engine.

For all that, students and instructors loved the old Avro and wrote many songs about her, the best of which is this adaptation of *That Old Fashioned Mother of Mine* which echoed around flying training schools for a decade or more:

Just an old-fashioned Avro with old-fashioned ways,
And a kick that says back-fire to you,
An old Mono engine that konks out and stays
When the toil of a long flight is through.
Though the pressure will drop and it loses its prop
And the pilot's inclined to resign,
I'll rejoice till I die — that I learnt how to fly
On that old-fashioned Avro of mine!
There are finer machines with much better wind-screens,
And whose pilots don't know what a dud engine means,
But my good old Avro can loop, roll or spin,
And there isn't a field that I can't put her in.

In peacetime few indeed were the fields in which Avros did not land, for, like the Jenny in America, the Avro 504 became a favourite mount of barnstormers and touring airshow fliers (and for the same reason — they were cheap and plentiful, some being knocked down at disposals sales for as little as £20). And like their American counterparts, not all the demobbed RFC pilots lived up to the dashing image they liked to project. One who wore immaculate white overalls with pilot's wings and bars of rank applied his insignia with strips of insulation tape, which went unnoticed by his admiring passengers in their excitement at getting aboard the Avro for their five-bob flips.

The touring joyriders modified their Avros to carry two and sometimes three passengers in the rear cockpit and found no shortage of takers for the draughty and uncomfortable accom-

Preparation for flight of the Shuttleworth Trust's rebuilt Avro 504K, with the Hucks starter's overhead gear engaging the propeller hub dogs for engine starting.

modation. In 1919 one company flew 10,000 passengers from Blackpool in a two-month period, each of four pilots, making 42 flights a day. Captain Percival Phillips, a buccaneering Cornishman whose St Austell-based Cornish Aviation Company's bright-red Avros were a familiar seaside sight during the 1920s and early 1930s, estimated that he personally flew about 91,250 passengers.

Sir Alan Cobham's flying circus, which flew nearly one million people in all, also used Avros. One of Cobham's most popular acts was a wing-walk by Martin Hearn, who would take an identically dressed dummy up with him and mid-way through his act fling it from the aeroplane while he ducked back into the cockpit, giving sensitive ladies an instant attack of the vapours and boosting the sale of smelling salts, no doubt. This piece of tomfoolery was curtailed after a visit to Ireland where an unusual percentage of the crowd comprised pregnant women who swooned clean away as 'Hearn' tumbled down.

I know of three airworthy Avro 504s. One, owned by Cole Palen at Old Rhinebeck, New York, is a replica built in England for a film with the unlikely title *The Bells of Hell Go Ting-a-Ling; Death Where is Thy Sting-a-Ling-a-Ling*. The film was never made, which is perhaps just as well, but the Avro still flies, complete with imitation Le Prieur rockets on its interplane struts and a garish yellow and black checkerboard colour scheme. In Canada the National Aeronautical Collection has an Avro 504K built in 1918 by the Grahame-White Company which was re-stored in 1967 by the Royal Canadian Air Force for Canada's Centennial Year and still takes to the air occasionally.

The only airworthy Avro in Britain belongs to the Shuttleworth Trust. It started life as a Lynx-engined 504N and was bought by Percival Phillips's company, Air Publicity, in August 1935. It was discovered on top of the stores at the de Havilland (formerly Airspeed) factory at Portsmouth Airport in 1951 and restored as a 504K by A V Roe apprentices for an appearance in the film *Reach for the Sky*. It is regularly flown by Air Commodore Allen Wheeler, himself a veteran of the Avro's era and a master of a gentle forgiving aeroplane which seldom bit those who abused it. It was its own reward for those who sought to perfect their skills and even gratified those who merely stood by to help on the ground – one engineer working on Avros during the joyriding years noted that a blast from the engine while young ladies were mounting the ladder to the cockpit could be 'most revealing'.

BRISTOL FIGHTER

She leans at her place on the tarmac
Like a tiger crouching for a spring,
From the arching spine of her fuselage line
To the ample spread of her wing.
With her tyres like sinews taughtened
And her tail skid's jaunty twist,
Her grey-cowled snout juts firmly out
Like a tight-clenched boxer's fist.
Is there a sweeter music,
A more contenting sound,
Than the purring clop of her broad-curved prop
As it gently ticks around?
Open her out to crescendo
To a deep-toned swelling roar,
Till she quivers and rocks as she strains at her
* chocks*
And clamours again to soar.

Thus lyrically did an anonymous Royal Flying Corps pilot eulogise the Bristol Fighter, affectionately known in service as the 'Brisfit' or 'Biff'. The aircraft started life not as a fighter at all, but as a reconnaissance aircraft to replace the Royal Flying Corps' obsolete BE2s. British & Colonial Aeroplane Company's designer, Frank Barnwell, planned to power the proposed R.2A (R for Reconnaissance) with a 120hp Beardmore engine, but when the Rolls-Royce Company produced its 190hp Falcon I engine Barnwell was quick to see that it was an ideal fighter power-

The Bristol company's most important contribution to World War I was the F.2A 'Brisfit', the RFC's first two-seat fighter. Here the restored Shuttleworth Brisfit is pictured.

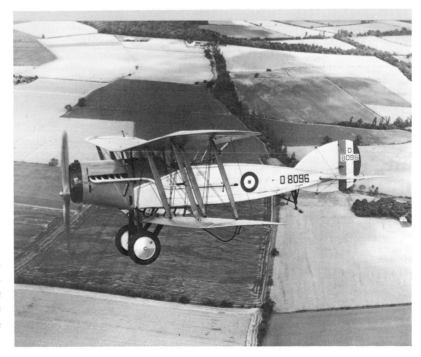

plant and set about rethinking the design.

The redesignated Bristol F.2A thus became the first two-seat fighter to enter service with the Royal Flying Corps, though its debut was far from auspicious. On 5 April 1917 six F.2As from 48 Squadron set off from their base at Bellevue. Near Douai they were attacked by five Albatros DIII scouts from Jagdstaffel II which were commanded by Manfred von Richthofen. Only two Brisfits escaped from the combat. The failure of the Bristols was purely tactical; their pilots, used to flying conventional two-seat reconnaissance aircraft, had used their armament defensively, forgetting (or more likely not even realising) that their big and seemingly clumsy biplane had all the speed and manoeuvrability of the German single-seaters, as well as greater firepower. The Bristol could be used exactly like a smaller scout, and once that lesson was learned it emerged as a formidable weapon.

The first 150 F.2B Brisfits had 190hp engines; later models had 260–275hp RR Falcons. Alongside the single-seat Pups and Camels they were huge, spanning nearly 40 feet and weighing more than a ton when loaded. Armament consisted of a single 0.303 Vickers machine gun fixed forward of the cockpit in the trough formed by the two banks of the Falcon's cylinders, firing forward through the geared slow-turning propeller controlled by a Constantinesco interrupter mechanism; and single or twin 0.303 Lewis gun(s) on a Scarff ring at the observer's position aft of the lower wing trailing edge.

The most effective combat technique was to rely principally on the fixed Vickers gun for attacks and regard the observer's weapons as a rearguard for fending off attacks from behind. The Brisfit provided an excellent gun platform with good all-round vision, except for directly astern and below, whence came most of the attacks resulting in early losses. Casualties among Brisfit observers remained high throughout the war without any apparent reluctance on the part of volunteers.

The Brisfit was the most successful British fighter of World War I, a fact duly acknowledged by the peacetime government, which awarded the British & Colonial Aeroplane Company (later Bristol Aeroplane Company) the sum of £80,000 in recognition of the aeroplane's contribution. The Brisfit formed the basis of the embryo Royal Air Force after the war and continued in service until 1932.

Altogether 4469 Brisfits were built; just one is still flying. It belongs, as do so many antique treasures, to the Shuttleworth Trust at Old

Warden. Brisfit D8096 was built in 1918 and did not see active service during World War I. In 1936 it came up for sale through the RAF Disposals Board and was bought by an ex-RFC pilot, though he never managed to restore it.

In 1949 the airframe, a spare engine and a Hucks Starter were discovered in a shed at Elstree Aerodrome near London and acquired by the Trust, which turned over the task of refurbishing to the original manufacturers. (The company planned to fly the old biplane before the King when he was to visit the Filton factory in 1950 to see the giant Brabazon airliner.) In the event, the restoration, which was done almost entirely from memory by veteran Bristol staff, was not completed until 1951, and the company's chief test pilot Bill Pegg was given the responsibility of flying the Brisfit for the first time in 15 years. He confessed afterwards that he had been much more nervous than on the occasion of the multi-million pound Brabazon's maiden flight.

The Brisfit is a gem. She does indeed crouch like a tiger, with a sturdy box fuselage tapering elegantly away to nothing at her elephant's-ear fin, the Falcon (which is the oldest working Rolls-Royce aero-engine in the world) tight-cowled save for the long exhausts which trail off aft of the cockpit, and the lower wing set unusually below the fuselage. In 1918 a Brisfit cost £1350; the Falcon cost another £1210. No one would put a price on the Shuttleworth's aeroplane today, but I can tell you that Vernon Ohmert of Ypsilanti, Michigan, has built six faultless replicas (but with modern 200hp Ranger engines in place of the Rolls-Royce) for the film *High Road to China*, and they cost $100,000 each.

Occasionally the Shuttleworth Trust uses the Hucks Starter to fire up the Falcon. Devised by the pioneer aviator and stunt pilot Benny Hucks, it consists of a Model T Ford chassis on which is mounted a rotating overhead shaft driven by chains and sprockets from the car engine. A spring-loaded crosshead at the forward end of the shaft engages a dog on the propeller hub. With the starter gear engaged the propeller is turned until the engine fires, automatically releasing the crosshead which is withdrawn out of harm's way by the spring. Ingenious, and it saves the arm muscles of Shuttleworth's mechanics who must otherwise form a chain of three men to swing the big propeller by the 'armstrong' method, rather like a one-sided tug o'war.

As you would expect (this *is* a Rolls-Royce), the Falcon runs sweetly and smoothly. You might not exactly be able to hear a clock tick in the cockpit, but the purring Falcon leaves you in no doubt that here was a very different engine from the spinning oil-spewing rotaries. No temperamental blipping throttle here, just silky instant response and full power whenever you needed it, though you had to monitor the water coolant temperature carefully and control it with the slatted radiator shutters at the front of the cowling.

In the air the Brisfit is stable, though heavy on the controls, particularly the ailerons, which did much to develop bulging biceps on RFC pilots forced to muscle them about the sky in aerial combat. The elevator controls were deliberately made heavy, for the Brisfit was designed to a specification calling for a maximum diving speed of 400mph (though it never reached anything like that figure, even in vertical dives), where light responses could swiftly have overstressed the structure.

The Trust's Brisfit is flown sedately, as befits age and rarity, but on a sunny day with the Falcon purring and her wires singing, she'll flash her silver wings and, in the words of that RFC poet:

Then up in a climbing turn
And off we sweep in a speckless sky
Till we catch our breath in the air Alp-high.
I wouldn't exchange my seat, not I,
For a thousand pounds to burn.

CURTISS JN-4 JENNY

This 1917 photograph of a US Army Curtiss Jenny shows particularly the complexity of the wing rigging wires.

Jenny was no lady. She was awkward and ugly, moody and temperamental. She was tattered and torn and down-at-heel; she sagged and she sighed, yet she was the sweetheart of a generation and the mother of an industry.

Jenny was the Curtiss JN-4 standard military tractor biplane, ordered by the US Army in 1914 in an attempt to reduce the appalling fatality rate among trainee pilots flying the Curtiss and Wright pusher biplanes then used for instruction. Surprisingly this aeroplane, which was to become the first mass-produced commercially successful American aircraft and the one which was to introduce flying to a million or more people across the United States, was designed by an Englishman, B Douglas Thomas, whom Glenn Curtiss persuaded to leave the Sopwith Company and journey to Hammondsport, bringing with him his preliminary designs for the JN-4.

The massive expansion of pilot training which followed America's entry into World War I brought forth unprecedented orders for Jennies, which were manufactured by Curtiss and six subcontractors in the United States and by Canadian Aeroplanes Limited. By the time the Armistice was signed and contracts cancelled, 6070 Jennies had been delivered and 95 percent of all Canadian and American pilots had trained on the aircraft.

The US Army found itself with an embarrassing surplus of nearly new but unwanted aeroplanes, which they offered for sale back to the manufacturers. Curtiss bought 2000, paying little more than 10 percent of what the Army had paid for them, refurbished them and advertised the Jenny as the answer to every airman's prayer, 'a bargain every aeronautical buyer must consider'. In 1919 a Jenny cost about $4000, but within a few years the large-scale dumping of surplus aircraft on to the market brought prices tumbling down and sparked off that romantic

and short-lived era, the age of the barnstormer.

The barnstormers were itinerant fliers, former army pilots cast adrift in peacetime with no trade save for flying and little hope of finding employment. As prices fell surplus Jennies and Canadian-built Canucks could be picked up for $500–$1000 (some even sold for as little as $50), and they came factory-fresh in stout wooden crates which served admirably as shanty homes when times were hard.

Across America there were millions who had never seen an aeroplane, a rich market waiting to be tapped. And so they came, lean hungry men in leather jackets and helmets and whipcord breeches who affected the ranks of major or colonel even though they had most likely never made it beyond sergeant. They would buzz the town to let the townspeople know they had arrived, then land in some friendly farmer's meadow and put up their signs: *Airplane Rides $25*. In the first year the pickings were good; the

best fliers could earn enough to pay for their Jennies in a couple of days, and if they cracked one up, well there were plenty more. Prices soon fell though, and by the early 1920s five-dollars-for-five-minutes was the standard charge, perhaps with a few flip-flops thrown in if the passengers had the stomach for them.

The Jennies grew tired, but they were undemanding old girls; a roll of linen, a can of dope and a strand or two of the farmer's bailing wire would keep them flying. The leaky old OX-5 engine which Curtiss affirmed was 'one of the most reliable' could be depended upon to let you down (in both respects) at least once a day, but a morning's work would buy a brand-new motor, and propellers were $36 a dozen, so the occasional crack-up was no disaster.

When the novelty of aeroplane rides wore thin, the crazier (or braver, depending upon your point of view) fliers took to stunting for the Hollywood movie-makers. The Jenny was a

These photos illustrate
some of the daring antics
practised by barnstormers
using war-surplus Jennies.

perfect mount; her wings were long and were held together with a forest of struts, kingposts, wingtip bows and wires which enabled a man to stroll about them in flight in a way which would have been impossible with a cleaner airframe, and the plain axle between the wheels made a perfect aerial trapeze.

Prominent among the stuntmen was Ormer Locklear, a young man from Fort Worth, Texas, who served with the US Army Signal Corps at San Antonio during the war. Heroic legends abound about Locklear. The most popular alleges that he was riding in a Jenny one day in 1917 when the trailing radio antenna which he had thrown out snagged on the tail bracing wires; Locklear is supposed to have climbed from the cockpit, squirmed his way aft and untangled the aerial, returning to the cockpit in time to receive the message from his commanding officer: *Locklear, UR grounded.*

Another version has it that he was instructing a student when the radiator cap on the OX-5 engine came loose. Locklear climbed up and over the centre-section, replaced the cap, then, as an encore, crawled down and sat on the axle while his white-faced student flew the aeroplane. Quite possibly all the stories are true, for within a few years Locklear was performing even more unlikely feats including handstands atop a Jenny's wing in flight, and plane-to-plane changes in mid-air. Locklear finally died while performing a spin at night for the film cameras when he became disorientated by searchlights and crashed explosively into the sludge pool of a California oil well.

Equally at home on the outside of a Jenny were men like Charles 'Smiles' O'Timmons, a one-legged one-armed parachutist who once filled in for a missing wing-walker. Unfortunately the heel of his artificial leg punctured the fabric on the Jenny's wing and he was trapped among broken framework. O'Timmons cooly unstrapped the leg and hopped back to the cockpit, to the horror of the watching crowd who could see his leg sticking up from the wing. He lost his trousers, too!

The barnstorming era was full of such characters making a quick buck. One named Wesley May actually bicycled along the top of a Jenny's wing in flight. The film cameraman shooting the event was so keen to get his pictures that he continued cranking the camera even after the propeller had sliced off one of his fingers. He went back to look for it later. And a mechanic working for Ivan Gates, a P T Barnum-style promoter who ran Gates Flying Circus, encapsulated those hard times with a cryptic telegram to his employer, who had warned him to keep all cables brief to save on costs. He had gone to the West Coast with pilot Swede Meyerhoffer, and Meyerhoffer had been killed swinging the Jenny's propeller. His message was brief, and to the point: *Swede cranked prop. Prop killed Swede. Send new prop.*

Rarely had any aeroplane been so mistreated as the Jenny, and not surprisingly no more than five are still flying, those faultlessly restored with not a trace of petticoat patching or bailing-wire bracing. No better tribute can I find than this anonymous soliloquy from an army pilot:

Old Jane, we rode the air together
In perfect and in bumpy weather;
We slipped and skidded through the sky
Those first few weeks I tried to fly;
None kind as you, none crude as I —
Old Jane.

We overdid topography
And rollicked through photography;
We had our turns and loops and spins;
We had our days of outs and ins;
We sinned our pleasant airy sins,
Old Jane.

First loves we were. No other ships
Can ever put you in eclipse;
New buses that I navigate
Coy, flighty, preening, bold, sedate,
Lack things I want, have tricks I hate —
Make me but more appreciate
Old Jane.

FOKKER TRIPLANE

Sir George Cayley, the 'Father of Aeronautics' first suggested the idea of multi-winged aeroplanes. Writing in *Mechanics Magazine* in 1843 he opined that 'in order to sustain great weights in the air the extension of the sustaining surfaces ought not to be made in one plane but in parallel planes one above the other . . . would it not be more likely to answer the purpose to compact it into the form of a three-decker?'

The first successful production triplane came from the Sopwith stable, designed by Herbert Smith. The first Sopwith Triplane flew on 30 May 1916 and so delighted was test pilot Harry Hawker with its handling that he looped it within minutes of take-off. It was immediately liked by squadron pilots when it entered service, and was put to good use by Flight Sub-Lieutenant Raymond Collishaw and his colleagues from B Flight of 10 Squadron, Royal Naval Air Service, the sinister 'Black Flight' whose all-black Triplanes destroyed 87 German aircraft in a three-month period.

The lesson of the Sopwith Triplane's extreme manoeuvrability in combat was quickly learned in Germany, where several captured examples were examined with great interest by representatives of all the major manufacturers at Adlershof, near Berlin, in June and July 1917.

The 1915 Fokker E III replica built by Doug Bianchi for the film *Crooks and Coronets* and used also in the BBC series *Wings*.

One of more than 60 replicas of the Fokker DR 1 built in recent years is this one owned by Leisure Sport in England.

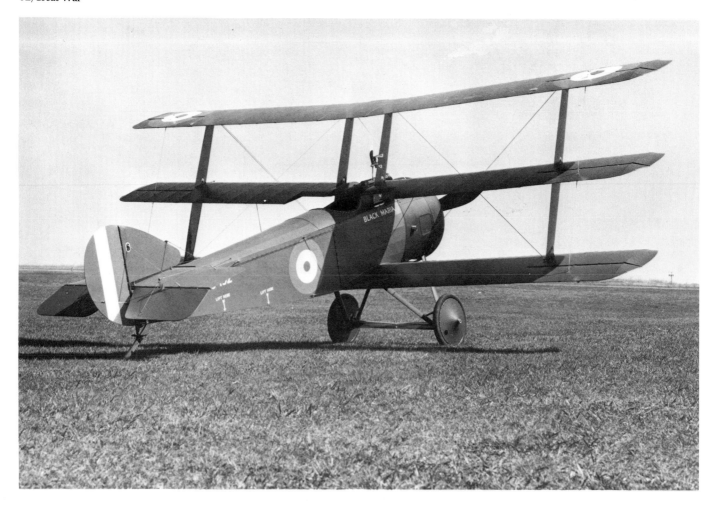

A 1916 Sopwith Triplane preserved in Canada and finished to represent one of the sinister RNAS 'Black Flight' machines.

Anthony Fokker, the brilliant young Dutch designer, had been given a preview of the aircraft earlier in the year and had travelled to the Front to watch the British triplanes in action. Consequently, when the German Directorate of Aircraft Production issued a statement in the summer of 1917 encouraging the development of triplanes (34 different prototypes appeared in all), Fokker was almost ready with his machine.

Controversy continues among World War I aircraft 'buffs' as to who actually designed the Fokker Triplane or Dreidecker. Fokker implies in his autobiography that it was he, but current opinion favours his assistant Reinhold Platz, a confirmed monoplane man to whom the triplane configuration was anathema, but who accepted the task forced upon him by his employer resignedly. Most probably Platz engineered Fokker's basic design.

The first Fokker Triplane, designated V.3, appeared at the Schwerin factory in July 1917. Whatever the influence of the captured Sopwiths, it was immediately apparent that it was no carbon copy of the British aircraft. The Fokker was smaller, more compact and had fully cantilevered wings with no bracing wires or even interplane struts. Early test flights posed questions as to the wisdom of omitting all wing bracing and the design was modified to in-

corporate outer interplane struts to damp out vibrations in flight and redesignated V.4.

Fokker's choice of engine for the Triplane was dictated by the supply problems which beset his company. Rival German manufacturers resented his Dutch nationality and saw to it that the newest water-cooled Mercedes and BMW powerplants were denied him. By chance during a visit to Adlershof Fokker had spotted piles of abandoned new 110hp Le Rhone engines which had been built under licence in Sweden by the Thulin company; they proved ideal for his aeroplane, though for the sake of Sweden's Allied contracts each engine was marked *beute* (captured) and neutrality was preserved in appearance if not in fact.

Orders were placed for 320 Fokker DR1 Triplanes and two of the first went to Manfred von Richthofen's Jagdgeschwader 1 late in August 1917. Leutnant Verner Voss, commander of Jasta 10 of the Richthofen Geschwader, first flew the Triplane on 29 August and scored his first victory with it five days later. Between 3 and 23 September 1917 Voss scored 10 victories with the Triplane and eventually destroyed 48 enemy aircraft with the type.

Richthofen, too, was enchanted with the Triplane, which has become synonymous with the Red Baron's Flying Circus and immortalised

by its leader who fought and died in one. 'It manoeuvres like the devil and climbs like a monkey,' von Richthofen reported after his first flight. Indeed it did. Devoid of drag-producing bracing wires, with a minimum of struts and weighing only 894 pounds empty, the Triplane climbed at the then-astonishing rate of 1131 feet per minute, and could top 10,000 feet in 10 minutes. Its featherlight pitch response and sensitivity in yaw enabled a skilled flier to outfly the best Allied scouts, though it was painfully slow compared to a SPAD or Sopwith Camel, and short on range. Given an expert combat pilot, the Fokker was arguably the best pure dogfighter of the war, a view shared by Germany's second highest scoring ace, Ernst Udet, who considered it 'the ideal fighting aeroplane', and liked the Fokker so much that he tried to have a replica built for sport flying after the war.

The Triplane's service entry was marred by accidents. On successive days in October 1917 Leutnant Heinrich Gontermann, Staffelführer of Jasta 15, one of Germany's prominent aces with 39 kills, and Leutnant Pastor of Jasta 11 died when the wings of their Triplanes failed in flight. All Fokker DR1s were immediately grounded for investigation. Poor glueing techniques and moisture had gone unnoticed in the haste of construction, leaving the Triplanes with wings

which had little more strength than soggy paper.

Modifications were devised, but the damage was done. Among both German and Allied fliers the Triplane gained an undesirable reputation as a pilot killer; although production got under way again only 173 aircraft had been delivered by May 1918, by which time the slow Triplane had reached the end of its front-line usefulness and was relegated to home defence duties.

Manfred von Richthofen scored his first victory with the Fokker on 2 September 1917,

Top: A Fokker DR1 Dreidecker replica built for the Old Rhinebeck Collection.

Above: Just one of the very many DR1 replicas, a home-built machine constructed to the most popular of the several sets of plans available, by American Ron Sands.

shooting down an RE.8 reconnaissance aircraft which made no attempt to take evasive action or open fire; its crew had mistaken the DR1 for a Sopwith Triplane. Thereafter von Richthofen retained his blood-red Triplane for combat even after his Geschwader re-equipped with Fokker's splendid Mercedes-powered D.7. Ever the hunter, Richthofen had the standard firing toggles of the Dreidecker's twin Spandau machine guns replaced by triggers mounted on the aircraft's control stick. His combat technique and superlative tactics are well captured in this report from a Camel pilot who was shot down by the Baron on 20 April 1918: 'I twisted and turned in an endeavour to avoid his line of fire, but he was too experienced a fighter, and only once did I manage to have him at a disadvantage, and then only for a few seconds, but in those few ticks of the clock I shot a number of bullets into his machine and thought I would have the honour of bringing him down, but in a trice the positions were reversed and he had set my emergency petrol tank alight, and I was hurtling earthward in flames.'

The next day von Richthofen was dead, killed either by a burst of fire from a Canadian pilot, Captain Roy Brown, or by Australian artillerymen, according to which of the traditional and long-disputed claims you believe. Either way, the lone hunter, toasted that night in RFC messes as 'our most worthy enemy' had died, and with his death began the German Air Corps' collapse.

The Fokker Triplane also had begun its decline and few seem to have survived after the Armistice. One was used briefly by a German chocolate manufacturer to advertise the company's products, but the last original Triplane — von Richthofen's machine restored after his death — was destroyed when RAF bombs hit the Deutches Museum in 1943.

No accurate plans, even, survived for the Dreidecker but infectious enthusiasm for the nimble little machine has encouraged antique aeroplane fans to build more replicas of it than any other World War I type. More than 60 are currently flying. Why so popular? Perhaps because the Triplane, immortalised by the legend of von Richthofen and his romantic circus of marauding hunters *is* the most famous of all the aeroplanes of the Great War, and certainly one of the most colourful. *Flight* magazine summed up the charisma of the Triplane back in March 1918 when one was first captured behind British lines. 'The Fokker Triplane is clearly remarkable . . .', it said, 'and offers a number of constructional details, some good, some indifferent, and some frankly bad, but always *interesting*.'

SOPWITH PUP

'We saw at once that the enemy aeroplane was superior to ours,' commented Manfred von Richthofen in January 1917 after his flight of Albatros scouts had encountered a new British machine. A rare tribute indeed from the Red Baron, but Tommy Sopwith's Pup *was* a superior aeroplane. More than that it was, according to one British flier, 'the prettiest to look at and the sweetest on the controls of all the aeroplanes of World War I', and one which was universally liked. Few aeroplanes attain true perfection; the Pup came close.

The Pup was designed by Sopwith's Herbert Smith and was the company's first single-seat fighter, following on from the Sopwith 1½-Strutter to which it bore a resemblance — hence the name Pup. (Officially the aircraft was known as the Sopwith Scout, or, in naval service, Sopwith Type 9901.) The prototype appeared in February 1916, small and compact, weighing just 790lb, yet with a Le Rhone rotary engine of only 80hp was able to out-perform its more powerful contemporaries thanks to a low wing loading and high power-to-weight ratio. At altitudes up to

17,000 feet, where other aircraft ran out of 'puff' and became sluggish, the Pup was still nimble and could out-turn the German Albatroses with ease, literally flying circles around them.

Armament consisted of a single fixed 0.303 Vickers gun synchronised to fire through the propeller by Sopwith-Kauper gear; a heavily padded windscreen was fitted to the gun's stock but proved totally ineffective at combating the gale of slipstream and propwash which would swiftly whip away a pilot's goggles if he did not fasten them tightly. Some squadron pilots modified their Pups to squeeze an extra hundred-feet-per-minute rate of climb out of them by stripping off all unnecessary weight; and that

miserable windscreen was usually first to go. There was little they could do about the vaporised spray of castor oil which the Le Rhone flung at them though. Daily exposure to this castor-oil bath was thought to be unhealthy. Experienced Royal Flying Corps pilots recommended regular doses of whisky as the most effective cure. Whether the scotch had any real therapeutic value is open to doubt, but it probably helped pass the time more pleasantly.

Not quite as original as its Shuttleworth-owned counterpart, this Sopwith Pup owned by Douglas Arnold at Blackbushe still has a proportion of its late-World War I-built structure.

The first Pups were delivered to the Royal Naval Air Service for the famous 'Naval Eight' No 8 Squadron, dispatched to the Western Front late in 1916 to reinforce the Royal Flying Corps, which had suffered heavy casualties during the Battle of the Somme. During three months of action Naval Eight destroyed 14 enemy aircraft and sent another 13 down out of control. Royal Flying Corps pilots revelled in their new superiority, too, as witness this smug little ditty sung in the Mess of 54 Squadron on the Western Front to the tune of *We've Come Up from Somerset*:

Oh we've come up from Fifty-Four,
We're the Sopwith Pups, you know,
And wherever you beastly Huns may be
The Sopwith Pups will go.
And if you want a proper scrap,
Don't chase BEs any more.
For we'll come up and do the job,
Because we're Fifty-Four!

The Canadian National Aeronautical Collection also maintains an airworthy Pup, seen here finished in the markings of 66 Sqn RFC.

An attractive study of the Shuttleworth Trust's Sopwith Pup.

Nimble in the air and not too heavy to manhandle on the ground, though it is doubtful that the Shuttleworth Pup is being rolled here by only one man.

What the Pup lacked in power it more than made up for in simplicity and lightness, yet it was sturdy and capable of sustaining severe damage while staying aloft. On one occasion, a Pup flown by Oliver Sutton – inventor of the famous Sutton Harness – collided with an Albatros DV which immediately spun in, while his grievously damaged Pup brought him safely home. In another incident a Pup was hit by machine-gun fire which severed an interplane strut, causing one lower wing panel to collapse. The aeroplane went into a spin at 16,000 feet. During the whirling descent its pilot made an attempt to climb on to the crumpled wing to force it back into position. Naturally he failed, so he climbed back into the cockpit to await what seemed like certain death, for there were no parachutes for RFC pilots. Incredibly he survived the impact, probably because the light wing loading of the Pup restricted the speed in the spin, and the flapping lower wing might also have slowed the descent.

The Pup retained its dominance through 1917 and was never bettered for sweet handling and sheer exuberance of flight. If it had any failing it was in firepower. The single Vickers gun was barely adequate, and if it jammed – an all too common occurrence – a swift dive for the safety of the British lines was the only course of action open to a Pup pilot. No 54 Squadron, which seems to have been a more musical bunch than most, had a song for that predicament, too, based on *D'ye Ken John Peel*:

When you soar in the air on a Sopwith Scout,
And you're scrapping with a Hun and your
gun cuts out,
Well, you stuff down your nose till your plugs
fall out,
'Cos you haven't got a hope in the morning!

To the Pup went also the honour of making the first landing of an aircraft on the deck of a moving ship. On 2 August 1917 Squadron Commander E H Dunning, RN, manoeuvred his Pup around the funnels and superstructure of HMS *Furious* and hovered near to stalling speed above her 228-foot flight deck while sailors grasped the machine's tailskid and bamboo wingtip hoops and hauled it down. A familiar photograph of the event shows deckhands clutching at the Pup as if trying to grasp an escaping canary. A few days later the Pup's engine failed at that last vital moment and a gust blew the aeroplane away from the clutching hands and over the side. The unfortunate Dunning drowned before they could launch the ship's boats.

A total of 1770 Sopwith Pups was built. In peacetime a two-seat civilian version appropriately named 'Dove' was marketed and one of them, restored to its single-seat configuration, still flies with the Shuttleworth Trust. Douglas Arnold, a collector of antique aircraft who owns Blackbushe Airport not far from London, has another which is part original, part replica, and on occasions you may see the pair of them fly together, agile as ever, their pilots sitting high in their tiny cockpits surrounded by a haze of castor-oil smoke and clutching at their goggles against those vicious darts of slipstream which tormented the boys on dawn patrol back in 1916.

Modern pilots are not quite so fulsome about the Pup's handling, for the gyroscopic action of the revolving Le Rhone rotary engine makes itself felt in turns. In one direction the aeroplane's nose rises, in the other it falls. Turns to the right are well co-ordinated, but to the left the Pup is unwilling to go without a hefty bootful of rudder, which says a lot for the skills of RNAS and RFC pilots who flew the Pup so effectively.

SPAD

'They were the best ships I ever flew,' declared Eddie Rickenbacker, the American Expeditionary Force's Ace of Aces, 'more impressive by far than any other airplane, any other automobile, any other piece of equipment I had ever seen . . . the ultimate aircraft in the war in which aviation developed.'

The aeroplane about which Rickenbacker enthused was the French SPAD scout built by Société Pour L'Aviation et ses Dérivés, a company headed by Louis Blériot who took over his rival Armand Deperdussin's firm Société Provisoire des Avions Deperdussin in 1914 after a financial scandal and contrived a new name to fit the wealthy silk merchant's familiar acronym.

Deperdussin's technical director Louis Béchéreau had been responsible for a number of innovative designs, including the 200km/h Deperdussin Monocoque racers with which Maurice Prévost won the 1912 Gordon Bennett Cup and the 1913 Schneider Trophy — the only occasion on which France won Jacques Schneider's accolade.

Béchéreau's first efforts for the new company were uninspired, but in 1915 he teamed up with Marc Birkigt, a talented Swiss engineer with the

Hispano-Suiza company. It was an auspicious partnership. Birkigt had just designed a light-weight aluminium-block water-cooled V-8 engine which promised to be more powerful, sturdy and reliable than contemporary rotary powerplants and around it Béchéreau created a dreadnought of an airframe which had great structural integrity but did not employ his expensive tulip-wood monocoque construction.

The first SPAD S.VII flew from Villacoublay near Paris in April 1916. With Birkigt's superb engine producing 140hp, it reached 122mph and climbed to 3000 metres in 15 minutes, far better than the Nieuport 17 which was then the mainstay of France's L'Aviation Militaire. Pugnacious and muscular in appearance, yet with a

characteristic touch of Gallic elegance and style (the long fish-tail exhausts would have graced one of Birkigt's Hispano-Suiza racing cars), the new SPAD was a machine set to stir the blood. In the tradition of making the best new aeroplanes available to skilled and experienced front-line pilots at the earliest opportunity the first SPADs appeared on the Western Front in September 1916, the second aircraft going to Lieutenant Georges Guynemer, the idolised young ace of Escadrille 3 of the famed Les Cigognes group, whose Nieuport 17s had been outclassed by the Germans' new Albatros D.I and D.II scouts.

The Albatros had two machine guns to the SPAD's single synchronised 0.303 Vickers, but the French aeroplane had other advantages.

A modern replica of a SPAD S.VII pictured at the Experimental Aircraft Association's Fly-In at Oshkosh, Wisconsin.

Close rib spacing, heavy trussing, doubled-up bracing wires and brass-bound interplane struts (additional wooden braces supported the intersections of the landing and flying wires giving the aircraft the appearance of a two-bay biplane) contributed to a structurally dense airframe. While it was heavier and less manoeuvrable than the nimble Nieuport, the SPAD was a steady and stable gun platform, could absorb enemy gunfire without catastrophic damage, and could be relied upon to survive the most demanding manoeuvres, whereas the lightly built Nieuport was prone to shedding wing fabric (and even wings) in high-velocity dives. The SPAD represented the best aeronautical technology at the midpoint of the war and was structurally one of the most advanced and interesting aircraft of the conflict.

The SPAD S.VII's reputation was quickly made and after an initial order for 268 machines for L'Aviation Militaire's *escadrilles de chasse*, by 1917 eight factories were producing the machine faster than any other aircraft anywhere in the world and SPADs were equipping the air arms of France, Belgium, Russia, Italy, Britain and the United States. Birkigt's admirable engine (surely the World War I equivalent of the Rolls-Royce Merlin?) had been continuously uprated to 150, 180, 200 and 220hp, and in all 5600 S.VIIs were built in France and others were manufactured under licence abroad.

At the suggestion of Guynemer a special cannon-armed variant – the S.XII – was developed which had a 37mm Hotchkiss cannon mounted between the cylinder banks of a 200hp Hispano-Suiza 8Bc *moteur-canon* and firing through a hollow crankshaft and propeller hub which were raised in line with the gun by means of a geared drive. Guynemer shot down four

Another view of a SPAD S.VII replica constructed by an American homebuilder.

German aircraft with a cannon-equipped SPAD, while René Fonck, the highest-scoring Allied ace, accounted for 11 of his 75 victories with the weapon, which invariably proved lethal but, being single shot, demanded the most accurate shooting, cool nerves and a steady hand to reload in the melee of combat. The Hotchkiss's recoil and vibration also caused problems and cordite fumes threatened almost to asphyxiate the unfortunate pilot.

Spurred by Birkigt's ability to extract ever more power from his splendid engine, Louis Béchéreau designed the SPAD S.XIII which first flew on 4 April 1917 and was immediately accepted by L'Aviation Militaire as a Nieuport/S.VII replacement. In the S.XIII Béchéreau outdid his own brilliance; the new aeroplane had twin Vickers guns and with a 220hp Hisso it could reach 138mph – fully 30mph faster than

its best contemporary rivals and 20mph faster than scouts which did not appear until the end of the war. A 300hp version the S.XVII, was developed but only 20 had been delivered when the Armistice was signed, for which, remarked one French flier, 'let the Boche be truly thankful.'

About 14,400 SPADs of all models were built, more than any other fighter prior to 1939, and had unprecedented orders from the United States not been cancelled when peace came and the aeroplanes left unfinished that number might have topped 25,000. Many World War I veterans rate Béchéreau's designs as the best fighters of the war. They helped swing the mastery of the air over the Western Front back to the Allies when new German aircraft threatened another 'scourge' and were instrumental in making the reputations of aces such as Rickenbacker, who scored 26 victories in eight months with the 94th Aero ('Uncle Sam's Hat-in-Ring') Squadron, and Guynemer, who called the SPAD 'a flying machine gun' and downed 54 German aircraft in one destructive two-year-period.

Guynemer, just 21 years of age, drove himself to the limits of physical stamina and courage, resolutely refusing rest periods. He disappeared on a dawn patrol over Poelcapelle, Belgium, on 11 September 1917. No trace of him or his SPAD was ever found, although an earlier S.VIII flown by him is displayed at Les Invalides, in Paris. 'He was our pride and protection. His loss is the most cruel of all,' mourned President Clemenceau when news of Guynemer's death was finally released a week after he disappeared. Guynemer's compatriot René Fonck also served with Les Cigognes, a fighter group second in fame only to Richthofen's Circus. During their first six months with SPADs Les Cigognes shot down 200 aircraft, and Fonck himself twice downed six in a day and once dispatched three so quickly that the wreckage of all of them was contained within a quarter-mile circle.

What was it like to fly the SPAD? Demanding, but also rewarding to those with the right touch. The lack of dihedral made the aeroplane sensitive in roll and a SPAD was never a 'hands off' machine; it needed to be flown all the time. Its thin-airfoil-section wings gave a good rate of climb 'like a Venetian blind going through the sky', one pilot claimed), and an equally high sink rate with the engine throttled, so that it had to be motored in with power rather than glided down to a landing. Control forces were light, thanks to pushrod-operated ailerons, but the famous movie flier and stuntman Frank Tallman complained that the cockpit instrumentation 'wandered amiably about the cockpit like a professor hunting butterflies'.

Tallman restored and flew a SPAD S.VII which his partner Paul Mantz discovered in the basement of a deserted California hotel, and also became acquainted with one of the aircraft's idiosyncrasies which tormented pilots of the French escadrilles; the header tank for the Hisso's cooling system was located in the wing centre-section just above the pilot's head, and perfectly positioned to spray him with scalding water should it be punctured or spring a leak.

Another American pilot who rediscovered the SPAD long after its glorious days was Cole Palen, founder and curator of a most magnificent collection of antique aircraft at Old Rhinebeck in upstate New York (see Chapter 5). Palen obtained an S.XIII from the Roosevelt Field Collection and restored it to airworthiness. It was Palen's first veteran machine and with no

experience of World War I biplanes (or any biplanes) he had to teach himself to fly it. 'Sitting in the cockpit is like sitting on a sled,' he says, 'with your feet out ahead of you on the rudder bar. You have to sit that way because the engine mount comes almost back to the pilot's seat and you are sitting under the engine mount.'

Palen came across another SPAD trait — a tendency to ground loop during the landing roll. One veteran American Expeditionary Force pilot described the SPAD's behaviour on the ground picturesquely as akin to 'a fat guy on a toboggan going downhill'. Cole Palen managed to tame the beast with a few white-knuckle sessions, but his SPAD no longer flies. However, an increasing number of S.VII and S.XIII replicas are appearing both in the United States and Europe. But while Béchéreau's fine airframe may be duplicated, modern horizontally opposed engines are no substitute for Marc Birkigt's timely Hispano-Suiza.

Probably encouraged by US air ace Eddie Rickenbacker's enthusiasm, a replica of a SPAD S.VII built in America in 1978.

GREAT WAR: A REVIEW

Left: The German LVG CVI pictured here in flight at Old Warden is a tribute to the important and dedicated restoration work undertaken by the Shuttleworth Trust. When the old machine, which had seen action against the Allies in 1918, was acquired by the Trust it was missing several vital parts, including the complete water cooling system for its Benz six-cylinder engine, all of which had to be designed and built without benefit of original detailed plans.

Below: The Deperdussin A-type 1912 racer was well ahead of its time in its aerodynamically clean monocoque fuselage and faired struts, and reaped the reward of advanced design by being first to exceed 200kph and winning the Gordon Bennett Cup in 1912 and again in 1913. Pictured is a replica built by the Salis Collection.

This worthy relic of World War I, flown regularly from Old Warden, was designed at the Royal Aircraft Factory and built by Wolseley Motors. The SE.5a was certainly among the best of the World War I scouts, despite severe criticism of some of the Factory's designs. The restored aircraft was in squadron service just before the war ended and after several years with Savage Skywriting and a long lay-up it was acquired by the Shuttleworth Trust and restored to flying condition by the Royal Aircraft Establishment, successor to the Factory.

Above: Last of the German World War I Fokker aeroplanes was the D.7, a replica of which built from original plans for Leisure Sport is pictured. The Fokker D.7 was the only aircraft specifically mentioned in the Allied peace terms as having to be handed over at once (though many were smuggled out of Germany to Holland before the occupying troops could take possession of them).

Right: A pair of World War I rivals portrayed in replicas, both built by Doug Bianchi to take part in mock dogfights at airshows and the like, a Fokker D III Eindecker and a Morane-Saulnier N-type Bullet. The Bullet was first to use a fixed gun firing through the propeller, the blades of which were fitted with steel deflector plates to prevent damage by bullets.

3:GOLDEN AGE

Previous page:
The WACO ATO Taperwing is a pre-war acrobatic biplane. The one pictured, owned by US college professor Bob Lyjack and, as can be seen, fitted with a very effective smoke-generating system, is much in demand for aerobatic displays at airshows.

Which was aviation's most exciting period? My vote goes to the 1920s and 1930s, the 'between-the-wars' years. It was a time for adventuring, for widening horizons and spectacular trailblazing, perhaps the last era in which a talented (or doggedly persistent) amateur could beat the professional aviator at his own game and thus write his name in aviation history.

After the 'war to end all wars' there was a natural turning away from all matters military. Service cutbacks drove manufacturers to bankruptcy; vast numbers of demobilised pilots found themselves without work. The only hope for survival was civil aviation, and thus the aeroplane became a vehicle for exploration, reaching out across the world. Oceans fell beneath its spreading wings, distant continents were days rather than weeks away, new unexplored lands were opened up, and communications revolutionised.

They were years of heady achievement, excitement and exploration, fired by names like Cobham, Earhart, Johnson, Lindbergh and Mollison. In this period too

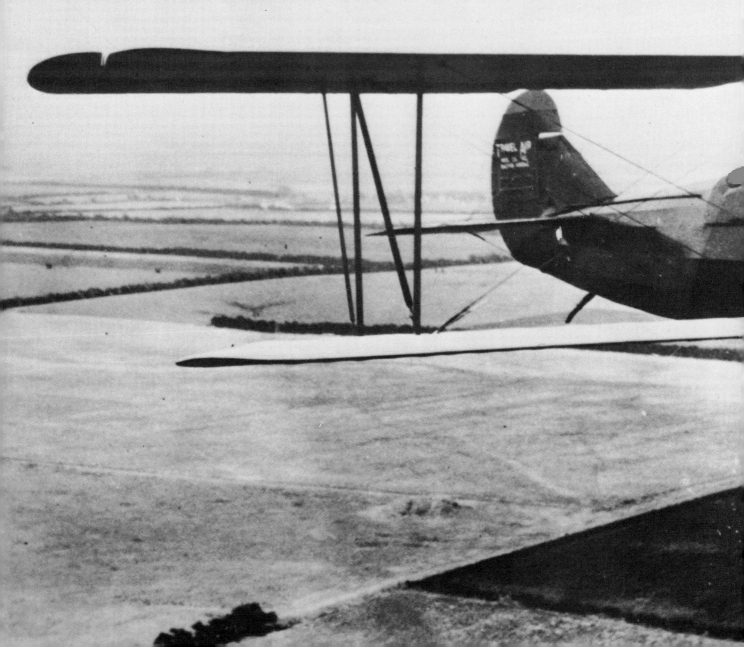

flying was established as a means of mass transportation and major air routes opened up. Even the ordinary man had a chance to fly as aviation grew as a sport and recreation, sponsored by far-sighted governments and manufacturers whose dreams of 'aeroplanes for all' have never quite reached fruition, and probably never will. Air racing and aerobatics burgeoned in Europe and North America with the great Schneider Trophy seaplane races, and the boisterous and bloody National Air Races in the United States, that mecca of free enterprise where amateur backyard builders with more courage than money produced aeroplanes capable of beating the best that the big manufacturers had to offer.

The aeroplanes themselves were the very stuff of history — Moths, Lockheed Vegas, Curtiss Hawks, Hawker Furies, Comet racers, Gladiators, Gulls and Gee Bees — colourful, glamorous, romantic names. Many have survived; those I have selected are inevitably a subjective choice, my favourite nuggets from the rich vein that was aviation's Golden Age.

A Stearman-designed 1925 Travel Air 2000 lightplane, a number of which are still regularly flying and product of the company formed by the Stearman-Cessna-Beech consortium that became the leading American planemaker by the late 1920s, when it merged with the giant Curtiss Wright company. The three original Travel Air principals thereafter broke away and formed their own separate companies.

BEECH STAGGERWING

Three 'good old' boys, Walter, Clyde and Lloyd, reckoned that they knew a thing or two about airplanes. So, in 1924, they set themselves up as the Travel Air Company in Witchita, Kansas, where they built sturdy dependable biplanes and vast single-engined monoplanes. Travel Air did nicely, but creative men are ever restless, eager for a change. Lloyd Stearman went first, followed a year later by Clyde Cessna, who saw his future in monoplanes. He was right. The Cessna Aircraft Company has sold more than 140,000 aircraft, every one a monoplane.

Walter Beech stayed on to see through the development of Travel Air's *Mystery Ship* racers which captured hundreds of transcontinental speed records in the late 1920s, then he too was away, moving across town in April 1932 to start the Beech Aircraft Company. Beech was a die-hard of the biplane school; he knew he had one last two-winger in him, one that would fly faster, higher and farther than the monoplanes his competitors were building. It would be his masterpiece.

And so it was. Designed by Beech and engineer Ted Wells, the Beech Model 17R was everything he had hoped it would be, and more; an exquisite four-place cabin biplane with a close-cowled 420hp Wright Whirlwind engine, streamlined enclosed landing gear and an extraordinary back-staggered wing configuration. It was fast, embarrassingly so for the US Army whose best pursuit ships were hard pressed to match its 200mph top speed. The Beech was, perhaps, the only production lightplane ever to have out-performed its military contemporaries.

That 1932 was a year of severe economic depression mattered little to Walter Beech, who had working capital (but not too much) from the disposal of Travel Air. Although he had proved that biplanes could be speedy he pressed the point by advertising an even faster and more powerful and expensive aeroplane – the Model A17F; it had a massive Wright Cyclone of 710hp, could reach 250mph, and would chase its tail in a ground-loop the instant the throttle was opened up for take-off if the pilot was unwary. Landings were all but uncontrollable, but an order quickly came in, and once Beech's engineers had solved the problem of welded joints breaking under the punishing vibrations

of the Cyclone, the aircraft served as an executive transport for a textile company.

Thus indulged, Beech began attuning his 'wonder plane' more closely to the market. Would it sell better, he wondered, if he installed a more economical engine of, say, 225hp, and arranged for the wheels to retract so as to preserve some of that sparkling performance? The Model B17L did indeed sell, and took on the now classic lines of the Staggerwing, an in-elegant name coined by a Miami airshow commentator in 1935 but never officially adopted by the company.

Perhaps one hundred or more of the 781 Staggerwings built are still flying, with many more being restored. Most are Model D17Ss with 450hp Pratt & Whitney R985 Wasp Junior engines, but you may still find examples of the Jacobs 'Shaky Jake'-powered Models C17L, E17B, and F17D (the so-called poor man's Staggerwings, which is a silly misnomer, for no Beech 17 owner could ever have been that poor – an E17B sold for $12,380 in 1940, a D17S for $18,870). Also to be found are the Wright-engined Models C17R and D17R and the G17S, the last production model which was still being custom-made to order after World War II. A G-model Staggerwing had the same engine as a D17S, but in an even cleaner air-frame with bigger control surfaces, more luxurious interior and improved landing gear.

There are some misguided people who will tell you that a Staggerwing is ugly. Pay no attention. A Staggerwing is a perfect fusion of curves and ellipses, as if old Walter rough-hewed it from stone and left it to the Kansas winds to smooth

A Beech D17S Staggerwing demonstrating the smokey start-up of its Pratt & Whitney radial.

and fashion to perfection. It seems to be going fast just sitting on the ground, leaning back like an eager greyhound straining at the leash. Step aboard through the single rear door, climb its sloping cockpit floor, breathe deep the heady tang of 1930s aeroplane, a pungent blend of worn leather, cellulose dope, oil, gasoline and a whiff of nostalgia. There is so much room — a wide bench in the back with space for three, and two individual seats up front which ride on rails worn silky smooth by generations of pilots. If your passengers were the nervous kind you could order your Beechcraft with parachutes fitted into the upholstery. There are courtesy lights and, if you please, wind-down windows.

In the cockpit an abundance of cranks, levers, taps, knobs and warning lights are placarded with varying degrees of advice, caution, instruction and consolation, for starting the Pratt & Whitney radial engine (*any* Pratt & Whitney radial engine) is much like preparing old steam traction engines. You do not just press the starter and go. You must coax, cajole and coerce it into life. Get it all together at just the right moment and the engine will never fail you; get it wrong

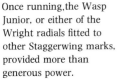

Once running, the Wasp Junior, or either of the Wright radials fitted to other Staggerwing marks, provided more than generous power.

and it will laugh at your incompetence and wait in stubborn silence for you to try again. Staggerwing owners ideally should have three hands for starting: one raises fuel pressure with a wobble pump while the others dance around setting fuel taps, master switch, magnetos, mixture, throttle, primer. Keep pumping, pause for breath, hit the starter and there's an asthmatic wheezing whine as one, two, three spatulate propeller blades flick over, mesh and disappear, as does the lower wing, in an oily fog of blue-grey smoke.

There is no sound quite like that of four hundred and fifty of Messrs Pratt & Whitney's thoroughbreds galloping a yard ahead of your knees at full power. Conversation is impossible, but the Staggerwing is off the ground in a trice, climbing effortlessly, almost loafing aloft with none of the straining 'come-on-old-girl-you-can-make-it' that you get with some antique biplanes. It will zip upwards at 1500 feet a minute and go five miles high. Thus, on a hot summer's day when roads are choked with automobiles a Staggerwing can bear you aloft betwixt its Spitfire-like wings to where welcome draughts

NC 80305

of cold clear air come rushing through those novel opening windows as you go sliding past towering, monolithic cumulo-nimbus clouds at 160 knots, like a shark gliding lazily through a reef. This antique aeroplane, nearly half a century old, is so cleanly designed that it is reluctant to slow even when throttled back; indeed the pilot's manual advises a 500-foot *climb* as the first course of action after an engine failure, trading excess airspeed for the safety of altitude — a technique which is usually the prerogative of the fighter pilot.

And even when you have finished marvelling at the way the Staggerwing enjoys the sky, there is one final delight. As the landing gear goes down there is a chain-over-sprockets rattle, a long drawn-out clacking like a clockwork motor running down or a ship dropping anchor. It comes from Walter Beech's effective but crude chain-operated retraction mechanism. The novelty of hearing its curious symphony should be adequate reminder to lower the wheels, but if not an interconnect prevents the throttle from being closed unless all three wheels are down and locked. It was a popular sales pitch in the 1930s to take a prospective buyer for a ride, stop the engine and land without dropping the wheels. Disaster? No, they just hoisted the

Staggerwing up, extended its legs and took off again. It must have been a very reassuring demonstration of the aeroplane's strength.

The Staggerwing is deservedly the queen of American antiques, honoured with its very own museum foundation in Tullahoma, Tennessee, where there is a flying example of each significant production model and a treasury of momentos of the Model 17s and the people who flew them — Howard Hughes; Jacqueline Cochran, who took one way up to 30,052 feet on a world record flight; Louis Thaden, who won the 1936 Bendix Trophy race from New York to Los Angeles at an average 166.06mph; Captain Harold Farquhar, an ex-Coldstream Guardsman and First Secretary to the British Legation in Mexico, who flew an early B17R clear around the world, 21,332 miles from New York to Heston, England, by way of Canada, Alaska, Russia, China, Siam, India, Iraq, Egypt, Tripoli and France, and inspired Beech's slogan: *The world is small when you fly a Beechcraft*; Amy Johnson, owner of the first Staggerwing in Europe; and Prince Bernhardt of the Netherlands, who used one for his personal transport in wartime exile. All those and many more have known the thrill of riding between those cockeyed wings which first flashed across the sky four decades ago.

This beautifully maintained Beech Staggerwing is one of many still flying; it is a D17S, most popular of the Staggerwing family.

B A SWALLOW

'Introducing the Safest Aeroplane in the World', says the faded yellow advertisement. Some claim! But I doubt whether the British Aircraft Manufacturing Company's immodest little slogan caused much of a stir back in 1935, when almost every light aircraft – even Henri Mignet's infamous *Pou du Ciel* (Flying Flea) which was positively lethal – seemed to have been applauded as the world's safest.

The Swallow dates back to the German Klemm Monoplane which was produced under licence in England during the early 1930s. In 1935 the assets of the then-defunct British Klemm Aeroplane Company were taken over by the British Aircraft Manufacturing Company, whose chief designer Marcus Langley revived and anglicised the machine. Some say unkindly that Langley had mislaid his French curves and had to work with straight-edge and square alone, hence the aeroplane's distinctive angular profile. The truth is that the revised design was more adaptable to rapid assembly at the firm's Hanworth Aerodrome works, close to the present London Heathrow Airport.

Few of the hundred-odd Swallows built have escaped the ravages of time and war. I know of only three still flying. One is owned by a friend, Don Ellis, who manages Sandown Airport on the Isle of Wight off the south coast of England. He calls it *Aeolus*. His aeroplane was built in 1937 and at that time cost £725, complete down to a fitted map-case. When war was declared *Aeolus*, along with many other privately owned aeroplanes, was given a quick coat of camouflage

Don Ellis in his Swallow *Aeolus* taxiing before take-off.

The *Aeolus* is one of only about three BA Swallows still in airworthy condition.

paint and pushed into military service on liaison or communications duties, or perhaps as a plaything for top brass. One militarised Swallow was converted into a glider, I know not why, and was to be seen dashing about the countryside towed by, of all things, a Spitfire.

This particular Swallow has a Pobjoy Cataract III seven-cylinder geared radial engine of just 80hp which slowly turns an immense airscrew of quite fearsome pitch. Swallows were also built with 90hp Cirrus inline engines, but afficionados of aero-engine sounds rate the creations of D R Pobjoy second only to the Rolls-Royce Merlin for pure acoustic bliss. They all make a unique and subtle *rattle-chug-pop* sound, like an ageing tractor ploughing an uphill meadow, but you will rarely hear it now, for only a handful of Comper Swifts and the Swallow have them. The prewar Short Scion Senior had four, and must have sounded marvellous.

The Swallow, like its feathered namesake, has long elegant wings, and they fold back alongside the fuselage for storage or, as was fashionable in the 1930s, for trailing behind a car. The pace and density of modern traffic make that idea a non-starter now. A pair of hinged flaps between the centre-section and outer wings swing up to give access to levers which disengage the wing locking pins. Then you dash smartly to each wingtip and pull on a ring-and-cable device and *Voila!* – a compact 15-foot span Swallow. Reverse the procedure – it is easy to do single-handed – and you are ready to fly.

But unlike its namesake, the old BA Swallow cannot count swiftness among its attributes. It cruises at 92mph and has an all-out maximum of 104mph. However, couple those speeds with a minimum controllable airspeed way down to around 25–30mph, and a solo take-off run of just 40 yards and you do have a flexible and agile flying machine.

The rear cockpit, from which the Swallow is flown, has just the bare essentials – magneto switches, tachometer, oil pressure gauge, altimeter, airspeed indicator, a big compass marked 'US Army' which certainly was not standard, and a spirit-level turn indicator, all set in a handsome polished wood panel. The engine has a self-starter worked by a bevel gear and lever arrangement connected to a ring-pull in the cockpit, not unlike that of a lawnmower. The Pobjoy starts with a great clatter of meshing gears, *rattle-chug-pop, rattle-chug-pop*, and while the engine speed builds up to over 2000rpm the mahogany log of a propeller seems to windmill around quite slowly thanks to its reduction gearing.

The immaculate handling of the Swallow and its vicelessness must have inspired confidence in those many pilots who gained their wings in them. *The Air Annual of the British Empire*, a splendid imperious almanac which loudly trumpeted the praises of all that was good, and sometimes bad, about the British aviation industry of the day vouched that the Swallow was the safest aeroplane in production and the easiest to fly '. . . will not stall or spin, its low landing speed enables the pilot to land almost anywhere.'

Certainly one Swallow, whose pilot had forgotten to set the brakes or chock the wheels before hand-swinging the propeller, took off on its own and flew around for 90 minutes before making a faultless landing in a field without so much as chipping the paintwork; and it survives to this day. One feels almost redundant sitting in the cockpit pondering that episode. And Pobjoy, the engine man, proved the point about the Swallow's ease of handling by buying one and teaching himself to fly it – a rare extravagance for a man who, in his early days, denied himself even a weekly cinema visit in order to finance his engine business. They say that when success came he had the floor of his assembly shops laid with Italian marble (and presumably started picture-going again). Personally, I would have been happy with the Swallow, which proves Aristotle wrong; one Swallow *can* make a summer.

CESSNA BOBCAT

If nicknames are a sign of affection you may conclude that the Cessna Aircraft Company's first twin-engine aeroplane was much loved, for you may hear it called Bobcat, Crane, Boxkite, perhaps even 'Double-Breasted Cub' or 'Useless '78,' but most likely 'the Bamboo Bomber.' Officially it was the Cessna Model T-50, whose design was started in the summer of 1938 under the direction of Clyde Cessna's nephew, Dwane Wallace.

At that time Cessna was not a major company, but a low-volume manufacturer of efficient high-wing single-engine monoplanes. By happy chance in less-than-happy circumstances the T-50 proved to be the right aeroplane in the right place at the right time and started a manufacturing dynasty which still dominates the private aircraft market.

Dwane Wallace flew the first prototype Model T-50 on 26 March 1939, and subsequently did all the certification test-flying without having a

twin-engine aircraft endorsement on his pilot's licence! After 100 hours of testing, the airframe was modified to production standard and put on the market at $29,675 – considerably less than Walter Beech's rival Model 18, but expensive enough to discourage all but well-heeled customers. Prestigious orders came in from the US Civil Aeronautics Authority and Pan American Airways, but it was the unpleasantness in Europe which was to transform both aeroplane and company.

As wartime demand for pilots soared, so too did the need for training aeroplanes, and the T-50 was selected by the Canadian Government for the British Empire joint training scheme. The first Canadian order for 640 aircraft (known as Crane Is in Royal Canadian Air Force service) was like striking oil for Cessna (who had manufactured only 250 aircraft in 12 years of business), and resulted in the Wichita workforce increasing eightfold in six months. When the US Army Air Corps also selected the T-50 as a multi-engine and bomber trainer, Cessna had two production lines running and was subcontracting manufacture of the aircraft's wooden components to Kansas furniture makers.

The Bobcat, as it was officially known in US military service, was powered by a pair of Jacobs R-755 engines rated 245hp for take-off and known universally as 'Shaky Jakes'. Many Canadian Cranes had fixed-pitch wooden propellers

which were disastrous to the aeroplane's single-engined performance when their draggy blades windmilled flat into the slipstream, although even the variable-pitch metal propellers on US Army AT-17 bomber trainers and UC-78 utility transports could not be fully feathered and merely went into high pitch, so that the aircraft's single-engine ceiling and climb rates were at best just 1500 feet and 40 feet per minute, and at worst, sea level with a 50-feet-per-minute *sink*-rate, all of which was good training for would-be heavy bomber fliers who treated an engine-out Bobcat with the greatest respect and thus sharpened their skills.

It was said of the Bobcat that any single-engined aeroplane with a duplicate set of engine controls would have made just as good a 'multi-engine' aeroplane – a far cry indeed from the original Cessna advertisement which promised T-50 pilots 'peace of mind for those who must have swift, dependable transportation regardless of terrain and most weather conditions . . . The Cessna twin will meet your every demand, for two engines are yours; either one can easily fly the T-50 fully loaded and speed you effortlessly to your destination without the other's aid.' . . . As long as there was no high ground between you and your destination, said cynical 'Bamboo Bomber' pilots.

Like many of its contemporaries, the Bobcat is styled much like American cars of the era; its

One of the few restored civil Cessna T-50s, the type that first flew in March 1939 and as the Crane 1 was bought by Canada as a twin-engine trainer.

single door shuts with a satisfying *thunk*, and the cabin has limousine spaciousness for five, complete with braided straphangs and felt trim. There is plenty of light from the overhead glass-house windows and a big windshield – through which rain used to leak in streams during bad-weather flight, demanding judicious caulking with wads of chewing gum which any experienced 'Bamboo Bomber' pilot would have ready. The 'Shaky Jakes' project forward of the cockpit like the boilers of two steam locomotives, their propeller arcs almost meeting at the tip of the snub nose. One sits atop a lumberyard of mahogany, spruce and plywood wing, whose mainspar one must climb to reach the pilots' seats. Old Bobcat hands claim you can synchronise the propellers by reaching around and placing a finger on the mainspar to feel the pulsing beat of the props. On demonstration flights Cessna salesmen used to give the control wheel a quick twist to show how the entire spar could flex quite safely . . . though they never did it more than once per aeroplane. The Cessna was certainly tough; a formation of student pilots flying AT-17s

across the Texas flatlands on a night training exercise espied the lights of what they took to be another formation ahead and elected to give their companions a start by sneaking up and flying underneath them. Too late they discovered that the lights were on five isolated radio towers . . . everyone walked away from the crashes.

In truth the maligned 'Shaky Jakes' shake not much at all, but harmonise nicely into a resonant rumble whose sound was described by writer Dick Bach as *MMRRrrrrowCHKkrelchAUM*. One cannot argue with such obvious talent for onomatopoeia. The 'Jakes' did have deservedly bad reputations for poor starting in cold weather; any pilot trained in Canada will respond with a string of expletives if one asks him about firing up a Crane in wintertime when the propellers had first to be hand-turned through coagulated oil which took on the consistency of quick-setting concrete even though the RCAF aeroplanes were fitted with round plywood discs which covered the entire front of the engines save for the carburetter screens.

In the air, with the mainwheels tucked up so

One of the very few remaining airworthy Cessna T-50 Bobcats is this highly polished specimen seen at an Oshkosh fly-in in 1978.

that the tyres mostly protrude below the nacelles to minimise damage in the inevitable gear-up landings to which retractable undercarriage training aeroplanes are subjected from time to time, the old Bobcat clips along at a respectable 170mph, stable as a Rolls-Royce cruising along a motorway, but burning rather more fuel – 30 gallons an hour, which is one reason why very few of the 5400 manufactured are still flying. These few have been restored to greater glory than ever was conferred at the factory and cherished in a way that would never have occurred to any white-knuckled 'Bamboo Bomber' student. Of the rest, time and the ravages of climate on the glued joints of wooden structures have decimated a once-flourishing postwar population of Bobcats, whose skeletal abandoned airframes may be found resting in forgotten airfield graveyards the world over, sad relics of the aeroplane which made a company.

D H TIGER MOTH

Having spent his early working life designing motorcycles, cars and buses it was perhaps inevitable that when Geoffrey de Havilland turned to aviation his dream was of 'aeroplanes for all' – cheap family runabouts which ordinary people might own. Although it never quite fleshed out that dream, his de Havilland Moth came nearer than most and its name is still synonymous with 'light aeroplane' in Britain.

The first Moth flew on 22 February 1925. It was of simple but sturdy construction with a plywood box fuselage and fabric-covered wooden wings. The engine was produced by cutting a war-surplus 120hp Airdisco in half,

Representative of one of the most numerous of the world's flying antiques, this de Havilland Tiger Moth is owned by a Compton Abbas (Dorset) club and is one of a few Moths still available for training hire.

resulting in a compact four-cylinder upright engine of 60hp named Cirrus I. A new Moth sold initially for £885 and was, according to *The Times*, 'an aeroplane for youth'.

Sir Sefton Brancker, then Director of Civil Aviation, evidently agreed for he ordered 90 Moths for the government-sponsored flying clubs which effectively started the private flying movement in Britain. Moths (the name was inspired by Sir Geoffrey's fascination with entomology) ap-

peared in successive guises as biplanes and low- and high-wing monoplanes, all named after British insects. However, one in particular was to earn a special place in the hearts of several generations of pilots – the DH 82A Tiger Moth.

Although it might be fitting to write of the Tiger Moth as a product of inspired genius and meticulous planning, the truth is that it was a child of serendipity, born of the very best traditions of table-napkin design and eyeball

Bigger and heavier precursor of the de Havilland Moth, this DH 51 *Miss Kenya* two/three-seater was delivered in 1925 and spent about 40 years in Kenya before joining the Shuttleworth Collection.

This privately owned DH 60G Gipsy Moth is one of very few flying examples of its particular section of the Moth family.

engineering, cobbled together piecemeal, an engine from here, an airframe from there, a little trial, a little more error and more than a hint of luck. By 1931 the de Havilland company was building the last of the upright-engined Moths, and a military variant was submitted to the Air Ministry as a potential Royal Air-Force trainer.

Civil DH 60 Moths were well-proved aeroplanes, but the Ministry was not happy with the centre-section fuel tank directly above the front cockpit, making rapid entry well nigh impossible for an instructor in full flying kit and parachute. But they liked the aeroplane generally and Geoffrey de Havilland's chief designer Arthur Hagg and engineer F C Plumb set to work on modifying the airframe in a tiny shed at Stag Lane Aerodrome, taking as their basis a Metal Moth mated to one of the new 120hp Gipsy III inverted inline engines from a Puss Moth. The obvious solution to the front cockpit access problem was to shift the centre-section forwards until the cabane struts were completely clear of the cockpit, but that put the centre of gravity behind the centre of pressure, so they swept the wings back by shortening each wooden rear spar. The result was the DH 60T which took the name Tiger Moth from the earlier DH 71 racer.

In September 1931 a prototype was dispatched for trials at the Aircraft and Armament Experimental Establishment at Martlesham Heath near Ipswich and back came an order for a production prototype, which was flying within the month. Thirty-five RAF Riger Moth Mark Is were ordered and in all 134 were built, including 20 manufactured under licence in Norway and Sweden before the DH 82A model was introduced in 1934 with an improved 130hp Gipsy

Major I engine and plywood fuselage decking replacing the stringers and fabric of the 82. It was this Tiger, the RAF's Mark II, which achieved the greatest fame. When production ceased in August 1945, 9231 Tigers of all kinds had been built, of which 8677 were 82As or Cs (the Canadian version) on lines at Stag Lane, Hatfield, Morris Motors Works at Cowley and in Australia, New Zealand, Norway, Portugal and Sweden. Perhaps 700 remain worldwide – a remarkable survival rate for an expendable training aeroplane.

And a distinctly military aeroplane, too, with cramped tandem cockpits and few of the niceties of its tourer contemporaries. It does have luggage lockers, which were very popular with RAF instructors off on weekend leaves, and climbing aboard is made comparatively easy by deep hinged door panels and the absence of the flying wires and hot exhaust pipes which were painful traps for the unwary on earlier Moths (though the long exhausts did an excellent job of heating the open cockpits.) The doors may be unlatched in the air to give more elbow room, but at the expense of raw blasts of wind which in any case seem to penetrate a Tiger's cockpit from every direction. It was, even by the standards of its day, an extraordinarily cold and draughty aeroplane and a good flying jacket was and still is desirable even in summer.

Thus helmeted, goggled and jacketed, you wrestle with the straps of the Sutton Harness which is a four-piece X-shaped affair designed not only to restrain, which it does most excellently, but also to infuriate the uninitiated.

Communication between occupants was never a Tiger Moth's strongpoint. It relied on the

Gosport Tube, a Heath Robinson contraption of tubes and earpieces (rather like, though less efficient than, a doctor's stethoscope) through which instructors somehow managed to hammer home the rudiments of airmanship to their ear-straining students. You can always tell a Tiger man by the minstrel-blacking of his face from the Gosport's rubber mouthpiece.

Trickier to fly than its contemporary, the Avro Tutor, intolerant of sloppy handling and having a knack of magnifying every little shortcoming in piloting technique (though never to the point of being dangerous), the Tiger was an excellent and surprisingly forgiving trainer, popular with instructors and the bane of students' lives. It was

Flying DH 82 Tiger Moth survivors are legion; seen here is a privately owned example restored in original Royal Navy markings.

said that if you could fly a Tiger you could fly anything, and those hundreds of thousands who gained their wings on them learned to *fly*, you may be sure. But although the Tiger's primary role was training, it was a most adaptable machine and served as an artillery spotter, light bomber, ground attack aircraft, maritime patroller and even as a target drone during World War II.

The 'bombers' carried eight 25-pounders on racks beneath wings or fuselage. Another scheme involved fitting trays under the rear instrument panel for stowing Mills bombs which pilots were supposed to drop down chutes in the floor. The boffins thought this a grand idea, but pilots pondered the dire results of live grenades jamming in the chute and the notion was quickly abandoned. Five Tiger Moth coastal patrol units were set up in 1939 at bases in Scotland, Northern Ireland, the northwest coast and in the West Country. They flew in pairs recording shipping movements and watching U-boats, their pilots tormented by freezing sea-spray from

which the airframe was protected by lashings of gooey yellow lanolin paste. If an enemy submarine was sighted they were supposed to fire flares and wait around for naval units to arrive and make the kill. Ditchings were not uncommon and the Tiger pilots carried a brace of pigeons in wicker baskets so that they could send a note of their position back to base. The birds were nothing but a liability, because the wood shavings provided for their comfort, loose feathers and a profusion of droppings were all blown back into the pilots' faces, causing sore throats and even more sorely frayed tempers. Incredibly one U-boat was destroyed as a result of their activities. Even more bizarre was a device called 'Paraslasher' invented by George Reid of the Reid and Sigrist Training School at Desford, Leicestershire. Pure *Dad's Army* in conception, the Paraslasher was a farmer's hand-scythe attached to an eight-foot pole projecting through the Tiger's lower fuselage. The Moth, it was thought, would fly among invading German paratroopers cutting canopies and shroudlines and further haras-

sing those who made it safely to the ground. It is easy to mock in hindsight but at the time a Nazi invasion looked imminent and ploughshares had rapidly to be made into swords, however makeshift. Besides, the prospect of being split asunder by 18 inches of cold steel travelling at 90mph was scarcely relishing, and the seemingly fatuous idea just might have worked.

Some Tigers even flew without pilots. The DH 82B Queen Bee, which appeared in 1934, was a gunnery target drone, the world's first truly operational pilotless aeroplane. Its guidance system was based on a two-axis autopilot which operated compressed air valves linked to the elevators and rudder through a radio receiver and relay. Most of the 420 Queen Bees built were operated on floats and controlled either from a ship's radio room or from a 'portable' console (it stood six feet high and weighed 1500lb) which provided nine commands via a telephone dial. Radio control was in its infancy then, and many was the operator who found himself being buzzed by his own Bee, or watched it disappear over the horizon, oblivious to his commands.

The Queen Bees also had a novel autoland device triggered by a bob-weight at the end of their 30-foot-long trailing aerials. When 'glide' was selected the throttle was partly closed and the biplane would glide down until the aerial struck the water surface, when the bob-weight would activate 'throttle fully closed,' switches off, stick back' commands, whereupon it would settle on the water to await recovery. Trouble began when several Bees were converted to conventional land undercarriages and flown from shore bases. With the uncluttered approaches of open sea the system was more or less foolproof, but as the Bees approached an airfield over hangers or trees the aerial touched, throttle closed, stick back . . . crunch. They soon got wise to that one.

Tiger Moths soldiered on in RAF service until 1954, when they were replaced by DH Chipmunks and there began an era of Tigers, Tigers everywhere as the elderly machines were sold off to clubs and private owners, often for very little money. Versatile in peace as in war, the Tiger served as trainer, glider-tug, crop-duster and airshow performer. Today, no longer the seedy workaday trainer, the Tiger Moth is a prized antique whose price tag runs into five figures. A thriving de Havilland Moth Club has worldwide membership totalling nearly 1000 owners and enthusiasts, and to prove that half a century on there's still life in the old girl, in 1978 Flight Lieutenant David Cyster flew his Tiger from England to Australia.

Were they the world's greatest trainers? Those who learned (and still do learn) in them would have it so. As with first loves, so with first aeroplanes. To the American his Stearman, the German his Stieglitz or Bücker Jungmann, and the Englishman his beloved Tiger Moth.

FORD TRIMOTOR

'Mom,' asked the little boy standing in line behind me, 'why does this aeroplane have wrinkles?' 'Because it's old, like your mother,' mom countered. However, that creased skin and the complexion of an old grey washboard have nothing to do with age. The aircraft was built that way.

We were waiting by a sign which said *Tin Goose Rides – $10* as the 'old goose' waddled up – a 1929 Ford Model 5-AT, the legendary Trimotor upon which much of America's airline network was built. When the man taking tickets agreed that I could 'ride up front and play co-pilot for another five bucks' I almost crushed his hand in my haste to press the money upon him. Not everyday do you get the chance to travel through time.

The first three-engined Ford aeroplane was the Model 3-AT which was designed by one William Bushnell Stout. Bill Stout was an eccentric inventor whose talent as an engineer was exceeded by his promotional ability. Smarting from the rejection of his torpedo-bomber design by the US Navy after one of *their* test pilots had wrecked it. Stout sent letters to 100 prominent American industrialists seeking financial backing for his Stout Metal Airplane Company. He asked for $1000 from each of them, promising in return only that they would most likely never see their money again. Amazingly he had soon raised $125,000, and the subscription list included such canny entrepreneurs as Walter P Chrysler, R E Olds (of Oldsmobile). Harvey Firestone, Marshall Field, and Henry Ford.

With Ford's backing Stout designed the single-engined Aerial Sedan, Air Pullman and 2-AT (for Air Transport). Ford ordered five 2-ATs for use by his company-owned airline ferrying freight and personnel between the Ford plant at Dearborn and factories in Chicago and Cleveland, and urged Stout to design a bigger machine, the 3-AT. It was a disaster. After a test flight in November 1925 test pilot 'Shorty' Schroeder summed up the 3-AT's future most succinctly: 'Forget it,' he told Ford.

Shortly afterwards the ugly duckling 3-AT

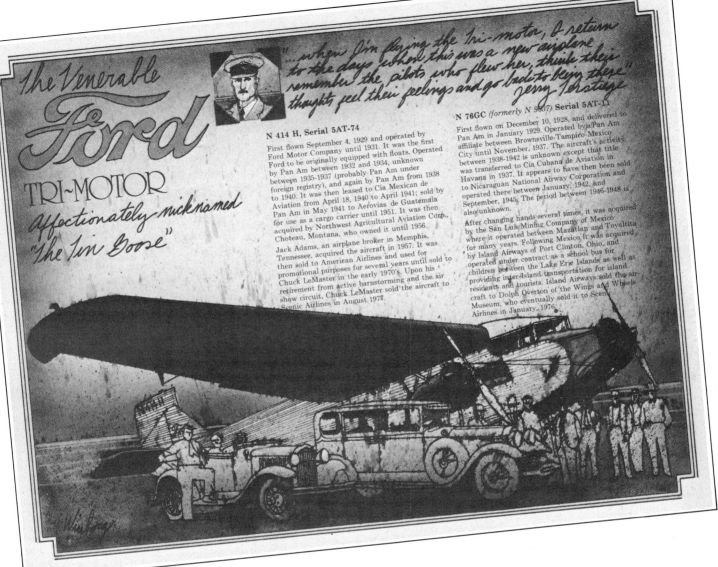

the Venerable Ford TRI-MOTOR affectionately nicknamed "The Tin Goose"

"...when I'm flying the tri-motor, I return to the days when this was a new airplane, remember the pilots who flew her, think their thoughts, feel their feelings and go back to being there"

Jerry Terstiege

N 414 H, Serial 5AT-74

First flown September 4, 1929 and operated by Ford Motor Company until 1931. It was the first Ford to be originally equipped with floats. Operated by Pan Am between 1932 and 1934, unknown between 1935-1937 (probably Pan Am under foreign registry), and again by Pan Am from 1938 to 1940. It was then leased to Cia Mexican de Aviation from April 18, 1940 to April 1941; sold by Pan Am in May 1941 to Aerovias de Guatemala for use as a cargo carrier until 1951. It was then acquired by Northwest Agricultural Aviation Corp., Choteau, Montana, who owned it until 1956. Jack Adams, an airplane broker in Memphis, Tennessee, acquired the aircraft in 1957. It was then sold to American Airlines and used for promotional purposes for several years until sold to Chuck LeMaster in the early 1970's. Upon his retirement from active barnstorming and the air show circuit, Chuck LeMaster sold the aircraft to Scenic Airlines in August 1977.

N 76GC *(formerly N 9637)* **Serial 5AT-11**

First flown on December 10, 1928, and delivered to Pan Am in January 1929. Operated by a Pan Am affiliate between Brownsville-Tampico-Mexico City until November, 1937. The aircraft's activity between 1938-1942 is unknown except that title was transferred to Cia Cubana de Aviation in Havana in 1937. It appears to have then been sold to Nicaraguan National Airway Corporation and operated there between January, 1942, and September, 1945. The period between 1946-1948 is also unknown.

After changing hands several times, it was acquired by the San Luis Mining Company of Mexico where it operated between Mazatlan and Tovaltita for many years. Following Mexico, it was acquired by Island Airways of Port Clinton, Ohio, and operated under contract as a school bus for children between the Lake Erie Islands as well as providing inter-island transportation for island residents and tourists. Island Airways sold the aircraft to Dolph Overton of the Wings and Wheels Museum, who eventually sold it to Scenic Airlines in January, 1976.

A section of the brochure describing the author's joyride in a 'Tin Goose'.

was conveniently destroyed in a mysterious factory fire, from whose flames arose the first Model 4-AT, designed by a Ford-appointed committee headed by Harold Hicks who had designed speedboats for Edsel Ford, while Stout was sent 'into exile' on a lecture tour.

The first 4-AT flew on 11 June 1926. It bore a strong resemblance to the Fokker F.VIII/3M (trimotor). Legend has it that when Commander Richard Byrd took his Fokker to visit Ford prior to his 1925–26 North Pole expedition, Ford had his men measure every inch of the aeroplane and told them, 'Build it like that, only in metal.' The Ford all-metal structure with that distinctive corrugated Alclad skinning was a strong selling point, made even stronger by the death of the famous Notre Dame football coach Knute Rockne when a wooden Fokker came apart during a storm in 1931.

The Ford Trimotor was the tool with which the airline routes were forged across the United States in the 1930s and 198 4-ATs and 5-ATs were built. Ford's friend Byrd, promoted Admiral, used one to make the first flight over

the South Pole on 28/29 November 1929; it rests today in the Ford Museum at Dearborn after spending a year buried in Antarctic ice. The Royal Typewriter Company had a special 4-AT which could carry 210 portable typewriters and drop 62 of them by parachute through a special rear hatch as part of a promotional campaign.

Even today you can still buy a ticket to ride in a 'Tin Goose', for Scenic Airways of Las Vegas, Nevada, operates a pair of the veteran machines on tourist sightseeing flights over the sparkling neon glitter of the gambler's mecca. If you get the opportunity, pay your $10.00 and go, because a Trimotor ride is an experience not to be missed.

My $15 seat is perched right behind one of the 'Tin Goose''s three 450hp Pratt & Whitney Wasp radial engines; earlier Fords had 300hp Wright Cyclones. When this one left the factory in September 1929 it would have cost $50,000. An airworthy Ford was recently advertised for sale at $1.25 million, and not all of that is infla-tion. This 'Tin Goose' spent three years on floats as a factory demonstrator before it was acquired by Pan American Airways and leased to Mexican, doing the rounds of South American operators and private owners in America until Trans World Airlines leased it from barnstormer John Louck in 1963 to make a commemorative run from Los Angeles to Philadelphia for the 25th anniversary of the Civil Aeronautics Act of 1938. The trip took 54 hours. It now operates with Scenic Airways.

Gone from the cabin are the wicker chairs, hatracks and reading lamps which some airline Fords had (passengers were offered cotton wool with which to stuff their ears and chewing gum to alleviate pressure changes on the eardrums when they boarded, and a stewardess on early Ford services confessed that she wondered why anyone rode at all, such were the discomforts of cold cabins, noise and nausea brought on by turbulence and the leakage of exhaust fumes). Instead the walls are covered with varnished plywood, the seats with leather. The roomy cabin holds 15 passengers and the view through the big windows is superb. But even today the howling engines outboard of the cabin make so much noise that stewardess briefings have to be made with a megaphone.

Up front the big leather-bound control wheels, which look as if they might have come from one

of Edsel Ford's motorboats, bear the patina of age, testimony to the sweat of a hundred palms. In fact the control wheels on early Trimotors came not from boats, but directly from the Model T automobile production line. Between the seats there used to be a long chromed handle, just like a gear lever. This 'Johnson Bar' worked the brakes; pulling up and back braked both main wheels, while application of rudder gave differential braking, so that during landing roll-out, a cautious pilot needed three hands — one for the throttle, one for a control wheel, and another for the Johnson Bar. A concert violinist might have felt at home. Toe-brakes replace the Johnson Bar now, and are used to pivot the Ford around precisely as we taxi out, nose held aloof as we pass a modern airliner, a DC-9. Who would like to bet that the DC-9 will be on the scrap pile while the 'Tin Goose' still flies? Not me.

At take-off the Ford is the world's noisiest aircraft. Apart from the buzz-saw rasp of three uncowled Pratt & Whitneys which defies all attempts at speech save for a full-throated yell, the metal skinning *boings* like a wobbleboard and the external control cables slap against the 'Tin Goose''s grooved flanks. I do not envy the

Another joyride-offering Ford Trimotor pictured at a 1978 Oshkosh fly-in.

men who flew them (at 90mph) across America. Such trips often took 31 hours of air-time. Truly a job for masochists.

And yet *I* would not trade my seat up here for a place on Concorde's supersonic flight deck. Here is the true stuff of pioneering, and as I sit with a big silly grin on my face while the old Ford lumbers over Wisconsin's Lake Winnebago threading her way back through the heavy air traffic of the Experimental Aircraft Association's annual convention, I am reminded of Harold Johnson, an old-time barnstormer who performed aerobatic routines in this elephantine bird. Johnson would snap roll the Ford at 800 feet, spin it from 1000 feet and do consecutive loops to ground level. His record. I think, was 27 in a row, after which he shut down the centre engine and did it all again.

No one loops Fords now — they are too valuable. We head back for Wittman Field at Oshkosh, slot into the pattern of brash faster-moving johnnie-come-lately lightplanes and touch, *chirp-chirp*, back into the 1970s. Another line of time-travellers are waiting, money in hand. 'Gosh, mom,' says our young friend, 'that was better than *Star Trek*!'

GLOSTER GLADIATOR

You can spot your girlfriend's house quite easily from 1000 feet. A tight turn or two to announce your arrival — yes, there she is in the garden, one hand raised to shield her eyes from the bright morning sun, the other waving frantically — now, stick forward, aim along the top of the cowling, speed building up, wires shrieking, leave it just a l-i-t-t-le longer, back on the stick and up and away in a zooming climb with 100 feet to spare, casting a glance backwards, grinning at her standing there with a hand to her mouth.

The CO has warned you all about buzzing, of course, and one of your friends died showing off to a girlfriend like that, but you're young and full of devilment, and a little diversion takes the tedium out of solo cross-country navigation exercises. Tonight you'll pick her up in your beloved 'chain gang' Frazer Nash and go barelling down the narrow country lanes with those sissy aero-screens down flat so that the wind

Shuttleworth Trust's unique airworthy Gloster Gladiator touches down at Old Warden.

can tear at her face and you can tell her that this is how it feels up here in your open cockpit.

Was there ever a better time to be a Royal Air Force pilot than in the 1930s, when it was said with some validity to be the world's best aero-club? Grass airfields, silver biplanes, their engine cowlings polished bright, colourful squadron markings snaking across wings and down fabric-covered fuselage sides, and impressionable young ladies by the dozen.

Romanticism? Perhaps, but such was the scene in early 1937 when the last great biplane fighter of the Royal Air Force entered service, heralding the era of the monoplane and the end of peace. The Gladiator was designed by H P 'Harry' Folland as a private venture, intended as a refined successor to the Gloster Gauntlet which, with the Bristol Bulldog, formed the nucleus of Britain's fighter force in the mid-thirties. The Gladiator prototype first flew on 12 September 1934 in the hands of Gloster's legendary test pilot Gerry Sayer. Like its predecessor it was an all-metal biplane, but one pair of interplane struts had been eliminated from each side, there was a cantilever Dowty undercarriage using internally sprung wheels and the Gladiator had four guns to the Gauntlet's two.

In production form the Gladiator was fitted with a fully enclosed cockpit – the first on a RAF fighter – and an 840hp Bristol Mercury radial engine which promised a top speed of 252mph. Even so, the Gladiator was outdated before it entered production, and was slower than some bombers then projected, but an Air Ministry order was placed in June 1935 for 23 aircraft as a stop-gap while the more-advanced monoplane fighters were being developed, and was followed by another contract for 180 three months later. Final orders totalled 480 for the RAF, 60 Sea Gladiators for the Fleet Air Arm and 216 for export.

The first Gladiators entered service with 72 Squadron at RAF Tangmere, Sussex, in February 1937, and equipped nine squadrons by September that year. They were a delight to fly, perhaps second only to the Hawker Fury in handling, though forward visibility between the cabane struts was poor and the accommodation was only marginally more cosy than that of its open-cockpit contemporaries, for there was no heating and at altitude the windscreen frosted over. Armament consisted of two Vickers and two Lewis guns on the first 70 aircraft, and a quartet of Brownings on later machines, one each side of the forward fuselage synchronised to fire through the propeller arc and one beneath each

lower wing in a streamlined blister fairing.

In all, 25 RAF squadrons received Gladiators and 13 squadrons still had them when war broke out, though they had largely been replaced in front-line operations by Spitfires and Hurricanes. But it was the old Gladiator, anachronism though it was, which intercepted the first Luftwaffe raiders over the Firth of Forth in September 1939, and on 17 October 1939 three pilots from B Flight, 607 Squadron, successfully attacked a Dornier Do 18 flying-boat and forced it to land off the Northumberland coast.

Two wartime actions are synonymous with the RAF's last biplane fighter. In April 1940 18 Gladiators from 263 Squadron left Scapa Flow aboard the aircraft carrier HMS *Glorious* bound for Norway, where they were to oppose Hitler's invasion forces. They arrived at a frozen lake near Lesjaskog on 24 April, planning to use the lake surface as a makeshift airfield. The Luftwaffe cut short that scheme by arriving next morning and bombing the ice, which was melting anyway, sending all but four of the Gladiators to the bottom. One has since been receovered and is exhibited at the RAF Museum at Hendon.

A month later, having already scored six kills during that very brief action, the boys from 263 returned to Norway, this time wisely operating from an airfield near Barduföss in the Arctic. In two weeks they shot down 26 enemy aircraft. On 2 June 1940 Pilot Officer L R Jacobsen of 263 Squadron, alone, took on six Heinkel He 111 and two Junkers Ju 88 bombers; he forced one Junkers to fly into a mountainside and shot down three of the Heinkels. But the flight was in vain. Five days later the squadron's 10 remaining Gladiators were once again evacuated aboard *Glorious*, and tragically on 8 June the carrier was sunk with the loss of all aircraft and most of the gallant fliers.

Two days later Italy entered the war and for three weeks Sea Gladiators flown by RAF pilots were the sole defence for the island of Malta against the Regia Aeronautica's bombers, a last glamorous episode (though not for the pilots) which effectively ended the Gladiator's fighting career. The names *Faith*, *Hope* and *Charity* (plenty of the former but not much of the latter) immortalised the Maltese Gladiators, but contrary to popular myth they were never actually carried by the aircraft.

Today you can see an airworthy Gladiator at only one place in the world – the Shuttleworth Trust's airfield, where former Gloster test pilot, Wing Commander R F 'Dicky' Martin, performs lovely lazy aerobatics, the Mercury engine hum-

ming like a well-oiled sewing machine. The Gladiator was one of two acquired after the war by former Fleet Air Arm pilot, Vivian Bellamy, a colourful character who then ran Hampshire Aeroplane Club at Southampton Airport (and also owned a two-seat Spitfire TIX, lucky man).

In 1950 he offered both aircraft to Gloster for the modest sum of £50 if they would take over restoration. The company demurred; they were heavy engaged in manufacturing Javelin delta-wing fighters for the RAF, but eventually a deal was made. When the Gloster Company closed in 1960 the aircraft was presented to the Trust, together with an unrestored Sea Gladiator air-frame, which is now being rebuilt at RNAS Yeovilton and is intended eventually to fly again with the other veterans of the Royal Navy Historic Aircraft Flight, namely the Swordfish, Sea Fury and Firefly.

GRANVILLE GEE BEE MODEL Z

The year is 1931. In a converted dance hall at the edge of the little airport at Springfield, Massachusetts, the Granville brothers — Zantford, whose friends call him 'Granny', and Tom, Bob,

Faithful replica of the Granville Brothers' masterpiece takes shape in California in December 1977.

Mark and Ed – have set up an aircraft factory turning out successful low-cost sports aeroplanes which have started winning races. But times are hard. The Depression is biting, pickings are few. The real money lies in the big unlimited-power air races held each year. Why not design an all-out racer for the National Air Races at Cleveland.

The Granvilles were farm boys turned aircraft builders, eyeball engineers, not one of them with more than a secondary-school education. 'Granny' had tried his hand at automobile repairing around Boston, and eventually turned to avi-

The Gee Bee replica, virtually indistinguishable from the original, in flight in 1978.

ation, setting up a mobile aeroplane repair shop on the back of an old truck. *You bend 'em, we mend 'em* was his motto. It was while fixing other people's aeroplanes that he got the notion to design and build his own, and thus began the Granville Brothers Aircraft company which was to have a brief, bloody but spectacular history.

Meanwhile it is summer 1931 and the National Air Races are barely six weeks away.

There's no money for the new racer, so out on the streets of Springfield go the Granvilles, dodging the soup-kitchen crowds, to seek out investors in their Springfield Air Racing Association syndicate, promising only that all prize money won by the non-existent racer will be shared out among those who had faith enough to finance it. They have plenty of confidence, if nothing else. Bob Hall, the company's chief designer whose

task it is to design the machine in a little over a month, sets to work, keeping barely a few hours ahead of the men building his aeroplane. They dash into his office to grab his blueprints the moment he is finished and almost before the drawing ink has dried the first wood is being cut and the first metal welded.

Incredibly the Gee Bee (for Granville Brothers, though some claim it was because their aeroplanes gave you the 'heeby geebies') Model Z was finished and flown for the first time on 22 August 1931. The National Races started exactly one week later. The aeroplane was based on the Gee Bee Model X Sportster which had placed second in the all-American Air Derby in 1930. The fuselage was shortened to just 15 feet and a 535hp Pratt & Whitney Wasp radial engine installed. The fuselage was widened so that it matched the diameter of the engine cowling, further accenting the Gee Bee's stubby appearance, and to compensate for the great weight of the Wasp the canopied cockpit was moved aft until it faired into the rear fuselage/fin junction. Painted yellow and black, the Model Z looked exactly like an angry pugnacious bumble bee. On its cowling it bore the name *City of Springfield* in honour of its sponsors, together with a drawing of prominent city buildings.

There was little time for test flying but designer Hall declared the machine OK and Lowell Bayles, a quiet slight young pilot who had flown the Model X in the all-American Derby (and who, with a $500 stake, was the Springfield Air Racing Association's biggest investor) was selected to fly it in the 'Big One', the Thompson Trophy Race.

By the end of the first week of September 1931 the Granville Brothers and the Gee Bee were famous. The Model Z took four firsts in National Air Races events. Hall won the General Tire & Rubber Company's Trophy at 189.545mph and a free-for-all event at 222.263mph; Bayles took the Goodyear Trophy at 206mph and zipped home in the prestigious Thompson Trophy race at 236.239mph to take a purse of $7500. The syndicate's members not only got their money back, they each made a 100 percent profit on the short-term investment.

The Granvilles were elated and went home to make plans while their rivals licked their wounds and wondered just who were these farm boys who had built a world-beating aeroplane in six weeks? During a speed dash at Cleveland the Model Z had touched 267mph. The world air speed record for landplanes stood then at 278.48mph, having been set by Frenchman Florintin Bonnet as long ago as 1924. It was

clearly within reach; the Massachusetts farmers could have the fastest landplane in the world. On to the front of the Model Z was grafted an immense 750hp Wasp engine with a specially made Curtiss-Reed propeller which left just eight inches of ground clearance.

A three-kilometre supervised course was set up at Wayne County Airport, Detroit, and during late November and early December Lowell Bayles made three attempts at the record, once topping 314mph, but technical troubles prevented him from achieving the four consecutive passes needed for an officially sanctioned record. On 5 December 1931, with the problems apparently cured, he set off to try again. It was to be his last flight, and the first of a series of tragedies which were to befall the Granville Brothers and their Gee Bees. As the Model Z dived towards the marked course from 1000 feet it reached 325mph and was down to 200 feet going through the course 'traps' when it suddenly pitched up, the starboard wing folded and it snap-rolled over and over into the ground and exploded, the flaming wreckage tumbling 200 yards. Every horrific second was recorded by the official movie cameras, and for years afterwards Bayles's terrible end was spliced into films whenever a spectacular aircrash sequence was needed.

Rumours circulated about aileron flutter and there were dark muttering's about the Granvilles' designs, but the cause of the crash was ironically mundane. The fuel tank cap on top of the fuselage had come loose and shattered Bayles's windscreen, stunning or perhaps killing him. In that split second he had instinctively pulled back on the control column and the abrupt pitch-up overstressed the wing.

The Granville's did not give up. They built more Super Sportsters, 'Flying Barrels', which earned fearsome reputations, but in September 1932 the world record finally was theirs, when Jimmy Doolittle flew the R-1 over a three-kilometre course at 296.287mph. Both the R-1 and the R-2 were wrecked in 1933 and another pilot, Russ Boardman, died. So too did 'Granny' in February 1934 when a new Sportster spun-in on a delivery flight.

The R-1/R-2 wrecks were rebuilt as the *Intestinal Fortitude*, an appropriately named aeroplane if ever there was. It killed pilot Cecil Allan at the start of the 1935 Bendix Trophy race. The last of the Gee Bees was the *Q.E.D.* (from the Latin *Quod Erat Demonstrandum* or which was to be demonstrated); it was entered in the 1934 Mac Robertson race from England to Australia by Jacquelin Cochran and Wes Smith. It retired at Bucharest, Romania, with engine trouble. Subsequently it was sold to the famous Mexican aviator Francisco Sarabia, who renamed it *Conquistador del Cielo*.

Sarabia seemed at last to have broken the Gee Bee jinx, for on 24 May 1939 he flew from Mexico City to New York in a world record time of 10 hours 47 minutes. Two weeks later, at 5.30 on the morning of 7 June 1939, the jinx struck back. Climbing away from Bolling Field, near Washington, DC, to return home, Sarabia lost power, stalled and flopped heavily into the Potomac River. The aircraft had not been badly damaged, but for nearly three hours it lay inverted in the mud while frantic efforts were made to extricate it. When a crane was finally brought to haul the *Conqueror of the Skies* out, Sarabia had drowned. Rumours of 'yankee' sabotage flashed around Mexico, but it was carelessness not subversion which had killed their hero. A rag, probably left inside the cowling by a thoughtless mechanic, had been sucked into the carburetter and cut the aircraft's fuel supply at the crucial moment of take-off.

Thus the Gee Bees' glory was but brief. Only one survives — Sarabia's *Conquistador* which his brother Santiago recovered and stored until the mid-1960s. Today it is displayed statically (no one would surely want to fly it) at Cuidad Lerdo in Mexico.

However, in 1978, in a corner of a hangar at Flabob Airport in California a familiar profile takes shape. Squat, fat, ugly, like an angry pugnacious bumble bee . . . a Gee Bee Model Z! Builder Ed Marquart was commissioned to construct a Model Z replica by Bill Turner, a Californian who sat in the original aircraft at Cleveland in 1931 when he was nine years old, fell in love with its unlovely looks and has hankered to fly a Gee Bee ever since.

With the help of Bob and Ed Granville, Turner and Marquart started out on the project in 1973 and ended up with a replica which is all but indistinguishable from the original, down to an exactly matched paint job and the little drawing of Springfield city hall on the fat NACA cowling housing the 450 Pratt & Whitney engine. Sadly the two surviving Granvilles did not live to see the aeroplane fly; Ed died in 1977 and Bob just a week before the first flight on 25 November 1978. Bill Turner has also had his share of scares in the Model Z, including a flip-over when the brakes failed on landing, but the replica has already outlasted the original, which must be a good sign that perhaps the half-century-old jinx has finally been conquered.

PERCIVAL MEW GULL

Form follows function, they do say. Edgar Percival's little Mew Gull racer proved the point; it looked fast, and was fast — the first British civil aeroplane ever to exceed 200mph.

Captain Percival designed and built the Mew Gull himself to test a new wing section. The prototype E.1 first flew in March 1934, but was destroyed the following October. A second aircraft, designated E.2, was built at Gravesend from the wreck and promptly won the first race in which it was entered when Le Compte Guy de Chateaubrun took the Coupe Armand Esters in France at 188mph in July 1935. Edgar Percival piloted the aircraft on behalf of the Duke of Kent in the 1935 King's Cup race, finishing sixth at 208.91mph, but this second Mew Gull was also short lived. Flying from Bordeaux to Paris during the Michelin Trophy event in October 1935 Guy de Chateaubrun became lost in mountain fog and was forced to bale out, and the aircraft was destroyed. October seems to have been a bad month for Mew Gulls.

Four more were built. When plans were announced in June 1936 for an England to South Africa air race in connection with Johannesburg's Empire Exhibition, three Mew Gulls were entered for the event, which was sponsored by South African industrialist I W Schlesinger and had prizes totalling £10,000. A British entry was to have been flown by Tom

After a praiseworthy restoration job, the remarkable Percival Mew Gull racer of the 1930s.

Campbell Black, hero of the 1934 England-Australia race. Ten days before the start Campbell Black took the Mew Gull named *Miss Liverpool* to Speke Aerodrome, Liverpool; a Royal Air Force Hawker Hart light bomber taxied into the racer, slicing into the cockpit with its propeller and killing Black.

That was an inauspicious start to a race which was to turn into a fiasco. When the competitors lined up before dawn at Portsmouth Aerodrome on 29 September 1936 only nine of the 14 original entrants appeared. They were flagged away at one-minute intervals. The two remaining Mew Gulls were South African owned; they were the white-and-gold *Golden City* flown by South African pioneer aviator Major Alastair Miller and the red-and-gold *Baragwanath* flown by Captain Stanley Halse, chief flying instructor of the Johannesburg Light Aeroplane Club.

At Belgrade, the first compulsory checkpoint, Miller's aircraft was refuelled with low-grade petrol which wrecked his finely tuned 200hp Gipsy Six engine. Halse reached Africa well ahead of the rest of the field but, suffering acute back pains from long hours in the Mew Gull's cramped cockpit and nausea from petrol fumes, he missed the aerodrome at Salisbury because of heavy smoke from bush fires and made a forced landing on the veldt during which the aircraft struck an ant hill and was totally wrecked.

Golden City was returned to its homeland and was bought by an enterprising young sporting flier named Alex Henshaw. Tragic Campbell Black's *Miss Liverpool* was also repaired for Charles Gardner and Captain Edgar Percival had the fourth and last E.2 Mew Gull as his personal aircraft for the 1937 racing season, when the three aircraft were the front runners in every event. Percival, distinguished by his ever-present trilby hat (which he wears to this day), touched 264mph in his Mew Gull — faster even than the best RAF fighters of the day and only 16mph slower than the first Supermarine Spitfires then flying and they had five times the horsepower of Percival's 210hp Gipsy Six II.

The 1937 King's Cup — the jewel in British air racing's crown in prewar days (although now reduced to little more than a procession of production lightplanes) — was nearly a walkover for the Mew Gulls. Charles Gardner zipped past the field to take the Cup at 233.7mph and Edgar Percival came third. Henshaw was forced to retire and spent the winter of 1937/38 modifying his aircraft with the help of Jack Cross of Essex Aero, who ran an air-racing stable at Gravesend Aerodrome. Cross was a masterly engineer who

tuned the Mew's Gipsy Six R engine to perfection. Rewards came quickly. On 2 July 1938 Henshaw won the King's Cup at a record speed of 235.25mph. That record stood for 29 years, to be beaten at last by a privately owned P-51 Mustang fighter in 1967.

Not satisfied with the premier air racing trophy, Henshaw again set about improving the aircraft with an eye to breaking the record set in November 1937 by a de Havilland Comet racer for a return flight from England to Capetown. The Mew Gull's fuel capacity was increased from 40 to 90 gallons, so that it was little more than a flying fuel tank and well over its normal gross weight, and Henshaw was crammed into what little space there was left. He took off from Gravesend Aerodrome at 3.25 on the morning of 5 February 1939 and reached Capetown, 5997 miles away, in 39 hours 25 minutes at an average speed of 120mph including ground

stops at Oran, Gao, Libreville and Mossamedes. After resting for 27 hours he set off again for home, arriving at Gravesend 39 hours 36 minutes later, alarmingly covered in blood from an inflight nosebleed. The roundtrip time was four days, 10 hours, 16 minutes. No solo pilot has ever made the two-way journey faster in any type of aeroplane. Henshaw had shattered the Comet's record on half the horsepower and half the manpower.

During the war Charles Gardner's Mew Gull was destroyed by Luftwaffe bombers while stored in Lympne in Kent. Edgar Percival's aircraft was used by firefighters for practice at Luton Airport, a not uncommon piece of official vandalism which decimated the ranks of vintage aircraft in the years before enlightenment dawned. Alex Henshaw sold his historic Mew Gull to a French owner in 1939 and it remained hidden at Lyons throughout the war, undiscovered by the occu-

pying Germans. It was found again in 1950 and bought by Hugh Scrope for one million (old) francs. Restored and heavily modified over the years it won the King's Cup again in 1955 at 213.5mph and continued to race until 1965 when its engine blew up during a practice race and it was grounded. Aircraft 'preservationists' bought the aircraft and, finding that they could not dismantle the historic machine to get it transported by road vehicle, adopted the simple expedient of hacking off its wings — a curious kind of preservation.

But the Mew Gull tale has a happy ending. In 1972 the dismembered remains were acquired by Tom Storey and Martin Barraclough, two members of the Tiger Club at Redhill, near London. Storey and Barraclough decided to rebuild the aircraft to its original configuration, no small task because the vandalising 'preservationists' had sawn through the wing's main spar and virtu-

Captain Edgar Percival, still with trilby hat, recapturing the thrill of the cockpit of his restored masterpiece 40 years on, in 1978, when it flew again in the Kings Cup air race.

ally the entire airframe had to be replaced. Tom Storey worked on the Mew Gull for six years; while other club members were out flying you could find him at the back of the Redhill hangar labouring away at the sleek shape. 'When is it going to fly, Tom?' we kept asking.

It flew again, restored to its pristine beauty, smooth as alabaster, on 16 April 1978. That September Tom flew it in the King's Cup air race, 40 years after Alex Henshaw's victory in the event. The handicappers beat the Mew Gull on this occasion though, and a mass-production American lightplane crossed the line first. It did not matter. Just being there was reward enough, and there too was Captain Edgar Percival, complete with jaunty trilby, sitting again in the cockpit of a Mew Gull and having himself photographed just as he had four decades before. Not one of the modern aeroplanes on the field looked half as sleek, as potent, as the Mew Gull, which (to the author) is an art form in itself, a perfect sculpture in wood, and surely the most beautiful of all British aeroplanes of all time, the Spitfire included.

PIPER CUB

Just as Geoffrey de Havilland's Moth captured public imagination in Britain, so in America the Piper Cub became the archetypal lightplane whose name fell into common use as a generic term for any small aeroplane.

The Cub owes its origin to two self-taught aeronautical engineer brothers, C Gilbert and Gordon Taylor, who began manufacturing a two-seat parasol-winged lightplane called Chummy in 1926 at Rochester, New York. Two years later Gordon Taylor died and CG began casting around for a new site for his business. The citizens of Bradford, Pennsylvania, offered a $50,000 investment and that soon settled the location, and a prosperous Bradford oilman named William T Piper bought himself a directorship of Taylor Brothers Aircraft Corporation for $800.

Piper was a shrewd businessman and a superb salesman. He was quick to see that the $4000 Chummy had little chance of success in those

Restored and privately owned Piper O-59A (later L.4) Grasshopper military version of the Cub, finished in original US Army olive drab.

depressed times. What the country needed, apart from the proverbial five-cent cigar, was a cheap aeroplane, and Piper urged Taylor to design such a machine. The result was the Taylor E-2, basically a scaled-down Chummy powered by a locally produced 40hp engine called the Brownbach Tiger Kitten, a highly forgettable powerplant whose sole claim to fame is that it inspired the aeroplane's name – Cub.

The effects of the Wall Street crash were still being felt, however, and in 1931 the company was bankrupted. Piper acquired the liquidated company lock, stock and E-2 for $761, gave Taylor a half-interest in the newly styled Taylor Aircraft Corporation as an inducement to stay on as president and chief engineer, and placed an order with Continental Motors for one of their

new 37hp aero-engines. This airframe/engine partnership proved more successful (though Piper and Taylor's did not – Taylor quit after a policy disagreement in 1936 and set up the rival Taylorcraft company) and during its first four years the company made small profits from the sale of 132 aircraft.

In 1935 further refinements were made, including a fully enclosed cabin and a choice of three different 40hp powerplants, and in 1936 a new Taylor J-2 Cub redesigned by Taylor's successor, Walter Jamouneau, appeared, powered by a greatly improved Continental A-40 engine. It was an instant success, truly a 'people's plane', a Model T of the air, and like Henry Ford's all-black motorcars, you could have your Cub in any colour . . . so long as it was silver. By August of

that year aeroplanes were coming off the Bradford line at the rate of 20 a week, fly-away price $1270. 'Pay just $425 cash and fly away in your new Cub . . . balance in easy monthly instalments,' tempted the Taylor-advertisements. And that included eight hours dual instruction from the dealer – enough it was claimed to send you safely off on your own.

Business was brisk in the first year, but in 1937 a disastrous fire razed the Bradford factory. Undeterred Piper bounced back again, setting up shop with a double workforce in a disused silk mill at Lock Haven, Pennsylvania, right alongside the local airfield. The renamed Piper Aircraft Company introduced the J-3 'New Cub' the following year at a lower price of $1249 (one model sold for a bargain-basement price of $995 as the world's first 'under-$1000 airplane'; a good J-3 Cub sells for at least $5000 more than that today).

The J-3 was offered with a succession of increasingly powerful engines, from 40hp to 50, 55 and 65hp, all four-cylinder horizontally opposed powerplants save for the unusual Aeromarine-Lenape Papoose 50hp three-cylinder radial, but it was the 56hp variant with its handsome new 'Cub Yellow' colour scheme and brown bear-cub motif on the fin which was to become the most popular of all. At its peak another J-3 Cub came off the mile-long conveyor-belt production line every 70 minutes and 1500 dealers were involved in worldwide distribution.

The Cub is a classic lightplane design, its high-wing slab-sided configuration instantly familiar

Ever-popular with flying preservationists is the Piper Cub and this representative, a J-3C/65 finished in Cub standard yellow, is one of thousands still flying.

to any youngster who has built a model aeroplane. Indeed, its structure is model-simple, with welded-steel-tube fuselage and tail surfaces and wood/aluminium or (more commonly) all-metal wings, the airframe fabric-covered and having the very minimum of frills. There is no starter or electrical system, a simple wire-in-cork-float projects from the fuel tank ahead of the windscreen to serve as a contents gauge, and cabin furnishings comprise a pair of rudimentary tandem seats and a canvas sling for baggage. The seats on early Cubs were even more rudimentary until Old Man Piper himself had to ferry one from Pennsylvania all the way across America to the West Coast!

Getting aboard can be a daunting prospect. The single door is in two horizontally-divided halves and climbing in requires a jack-knife posture while backing and twisting around, at the same time swinging a leg over the control column and avoiding standing on the lift-struts. Champion gymnasts and limbo dancers have no problems; lesser mortals invariably leave a leg dangling foolishly outside on their first attempt. Flying controls are duplicated, as are the tiny heelbrakes (J-3s were the first Cubs to have brakes and steerable tailwheels, earlier models having just a tailskid), but only the front position has instruments and since the aeroplane must be soloed from the rear seat you must stretch forward to reset the altimeter when flying alone. The pilot's manual sagely advises that if seatbelts are used to lash the control columns when the aircraft is parked, then both must be untied before flight. 'Attempting to take off with a stick tied back will result in a spectacular rate of climb followed by an equally spectacular return to earth,' it says, adding superfluously, 'This kind of thing could spoil your whole day.'

Sales literature made great play of the machine's single-handed operational capability, for by standing behind the engine with the door open it is possible both to reach the engine controls *and* swing the propeller over yourself, a practice which has undoubtedly resulted in many a pilotless take-off. Two Canadian trappers returning from a hunting trip in the frozen north reputedly saved themselves from a cold death when their Cub's engine stopped by stepping out onto the landing gear in flight and hand-swinging the propeller, and a young British lady pilot is said to have performed a similar feat over the North Sea.

Take-off is a rapid affair, breaking ground at around 38mph, and with a field 1000 feet in length a Cub owner can 'baby' his engine and use only 40 of the available 65hp to get off. The cabin is noisy, particularly at the Cub's leisurely maximum speed of 90mph when a barrage of engine noise, vibration and slipstream bears hard on the ears, and at normal cruise speeds, around 70mph, the Cub is not an aeroplane to go dashing hither and yon; in a headwind cars will be overtaking it.

Nonetheless the Cub will fly 220 miles on a full tank and for relaxing journeys with frequent stops it can make a delightful husband-and-wife tourer. One friend of mine who owns a Cub flies off up-country for long weekends, taking along a couple of overnight bags and a picnic hamper, and stops off en route at farms for a bite to eat and a stretch of the legs. His Cub has no radio or navigation aids except a compass, but it is so inherently stable that it will fly hands-off indefinitely and is a natural for 'eyeball' navigation — just drop down to 500 feet or so, open the door and navigate by road map. With a binocular-equipped passenger one might do without maps altogether, and pick one's way by roadsigns.

If lack of speed is the Cub's weakness, slow-speed handling must be its forte. At 45mph it putters along nicely; ease the stick back and the airspeed falls all the way down towards 30mph and still it hangs there, clawing the air and refusing to stall, even when you try hard. Small wonder that it was popular as an Army observation aeroplane. Grasshoppers, they called them, allegedly because a crusty old cavalry brigade commander in the US Army remarked to a civilian pilot taking part in the 1941 Third Army manoeuvres held in El Paso, Texas, that his Cub had looked 'just like a goddam grasshopper out there on the boondocks'.

Thereafter the US Army ordered nearly 6000 J-3s for observation duties and they served in every major war theatre up to Korea. Over 1000 were painted up in D-Day stripes and flown from England to France to support the Allied invasion in 1944, where they splashed their way around waterlogged Normandy fields, through snow flurries in the Ardennes and cruised from deserted German autobahns. Even before Pearl Harbor the Cub played its part when 49 silver-painted J-3s (one for each state of the union and one for Piper) swarmed into New York's La Guardia Airport bearing Royal Air Force roundels and the names 'Flitfire' as part of a fund-raising campaign for the RAF Benevolent Fund.

Seldom has any aeroplane been so used (and abused) as the Cub. Few indeed are the parts of the globe in which they have not operated, in civilian or military guise, from dirt strips, lakes, roads, glaciers, carrier decks, even from special platforms on tank landing craft, trucks, cars and trains. Cubs have alighted on endless combinations of wheels, bogies, skis, floats, hydrofoils, inflatable pontoons and caterpillar tracks. There have been low-wing Cubs, mid-wing Cubs, clipped-wing Cubs, biplane Cubs, Cubs with radial engines, twin engines, even a Cub with no engine at all – the TG-8 glider trainer in which unfortunate GIs were given rudimentary flying instruction before being sent off to ferry overladen troop carriers into the battle-torn fields of Europe. Tell me you have seen them on flanged wheels flying off railway tracks and I will not doubt you. Cubs are like that.

Then there was the Cub Composite: one J-3 mounted atop the other for a Minnesota airshow act, and two others were joined together Twin Mustang-style. Zaniest of all perhaps was *Mr Bones*, a J-3 owned by American airshow performer Cliff Winters which was nothing more or less than a bare fuselage frame without fabric,

doors, cowlings, windscreen and just about everything else, topped off with a pair of clipped wings with scalloped trailing edges, the whole thing decorated in multicoloured polkadots.

Piper built 14,000 125 J-3 Cubs, but the total number of Cub derivatives manufactured is three times that number, and amazingly, the airframe – albeit much modified – is still in production at Lock Haven as the PA-18 Super Cub 150 which is a perennial favourite of farmers, bush-fliers and other workaday pilots nearly half-a-century after the first Cub appeared. And a company in Wisconsin markets complete do-it-yourself kits for J-3 replicas, giving Taylor and Jamouneau's wonderfully timely design a further lease of life. Many thousands of Cubs are still flying, giving extraordinary economy to operation in these inflated times (at economy cruise speed a Cub burns less than three gallons of fuel an hour). It is, as William Piper's son Tony puts it, 'a naturally darn good flying machine'.

A civil J-3C Cub restored and owned by British Airways Captain Alan Chalkley flying over Buckinghamshire.

STEARMAN KAYDET

They would be lined up as far as the eye could see, seried ranks of chrome yellow wings and blue fuselages, rudders striped red, white and blue like Old Glory, ranged in military precision, the points of their white star markings precisely aligned. You knew all about military precision. Hours, days, weeks of it, around and around the parade ground, drilling until you were nearly drilled into the ground. 'Puff that chest out! Straighten those shoulders! Mister, I wanna see that back like a ramrod! Suck in that stomach! Son, were you born awkward, or did you grow that way?' You took it all, obeyed nonsensical orders without raising an eyebrow, and doubled around the barracks, silently cursing the Army and just longing for the day when you could get on with doing what you were there for — learning to fly.

The great day came, and you trooped out with your instructor to that yellow and blue biplane which one day you would look back on fondly as your *alma mater*. It was called a Stearman, though the military — as they always do — had their own name: PT-17, or Kaydet. The Navy called theirs N2Ss officially, 'Yellow Perils' colloquially. Yellow because of their colour and perils because of the need to stay well clear of the swarms of student pilots to whom they were classrooms of the air.

The Kaydet looked like an aeroplane should — sturdy and tough, with a big uncowled radial engine, a hefty long-stroke undercarriage to absorb the punishment meted out by the less than tender mercies of rookie fliers and big roomy cockpits. You have been comforted to learn that no one had ever succeeded in breaking a Stearman apart in the air, though one bored Air Corps instructor had once put one into a terminal-velocity dive and suddenly pulled up, just to see when the wings would come off. He did not need

his parachute. The Kaydet stayed together, though the cadet in the front seat went to pieces.

Instructors did odd things when they got bored, which was often. They'd climb out of the cockpit and stand on the wingroot. A sudden tap on the pupil's shoulder at 5000 feet could be alarming. A favourite ploy with nervous cadets was to slip out the quick-release pin on the control column in the instructor's cockpit and made a grand gesture of throwing the stick overboard. 'OK son, you got it now.' One student panicked and did the same thing with his stick; luckily the instructor was an old hand at throwing them in at the deep end and had brought along a short length of broomhandle which he inserted in the empty socket and flew the aeroplane

Star of many American airshows is the Stearman PT-17 Kaydet. In this picture is Wayne Pearce's *Ole Smokey*, nearer the camera, and Bob and Pat Wagner's Kaydet in a duet display.

home, before sending his twitching student back by road to look for the discarded control columns.

The Stearman company dated back to 1919 when a rich oilman named Jake Moellendick put up $30,000 to bring a talented aircraft designer called E M 'Matty' Laird to the Kansas cow-town of Wichita, now the self-styled 'Aviation Capital of the World'. With Laird came Buck Weaver (who later started the Waco company), Walter Beech and Lloyd Carlton Stearman. The group stayed together until 1922 building Laird Swallow biplanes before Weaver and Laird left. Beech and Stearman stayed on until they too had a dispute with Moellendick and teamed up with Clyde Cessna to form the Travel Air Manufacturing Company, whence Stearman himself departed in 1926 to establish his own company in California. Within a year Stearman, whose motto was *Dedicated to the Discriminating Buyer*, was back in Wichita and in 1929 his company became part of the giant United Aircraft & Transport Corporation, which also owned United Airlines, Boeing, Sikorsky, Vought, Hamilton Standard and Pratt & Whitney.

Paradoxically Lloyd Stearman had no part in

the creation of the aeroplane which was to make a legend of his name. He left the company which he had founded but no longer controlled in 1932. Two years later designers Harold Zipp and Jack Clark created the first Stearman Model 70 which was evaluated by the US Army and Navy. The Navy ordered 61 production NS-1s; the Army demurred but eventually bought 26 PT-13 variants of the improved Model 75. It was the first time that the two services had ever agreed on a common aircraft type (or on virtually any other subject, for that matter). The Stearman Company was by then a division of Boeing, and strictly speaking a 'Stearman' is not a Stearman at all, but a Boeing though no one ever calls it that. Boeings, as any self-respecting Stearman man will be quick to tell you, are noisy smelly jet airliners; the Stearman is a *real* airplane.

The Army and Navy followed up their orders with further contracts for Lycoming and Jacobs-engined PT-13s and PT-18s and Continental-powered N2Ss, but the most popular of all models was the 220hp Continental-engined PT-17 Kaydet which was supplied to the US forces and to Argentina, Bolivia, Canada, China, Colombia, Cuba, Guatemala, Dominica, Peru, the Philippines and Venezuela. Production of all Stearman Kaydet types totalled 10,346 including spare airframes. The last aircraft left the line in February 1945 and was used by Boeing-Wichita for publicity until 1958 when 'the last of the many' was donated to the USAF Museum at Wright-Patterson Air Force base near Dayton, Ohio.

After the war more than 5000 surplus Stearmans found their way to civil customers, sold off for as little as $300 apiece from surplus storage depots like the one at Ogden, Utah, where hundreds of PT-17s and N2Ss were stacked on their noses in hangars, crammed in so tightly that you could scarcely put a foot between them. The Stearman found a ready and valuable peacetime application as the backbone of America's agricultural aviation fleet — crop-dusting and spraying — and US farmers owe a great debt to the tough design which proved easily adaptable to more powerful engines and heavy chemical hoppers.

How many Stearmans survive? It is hard to say for sure. Perhaps 1500 are still flying, but there may be another two or three thousand stored away, quietly awaiting the day when they might serve again. Dick Reade, who runs the Mid-Continent Aircraft Corporation down in Hayti, Missouri, has stockpiles of airframes which he rebuilds to order. He has been doing it these past 30 years and prides himself that his is the only place in the world where you can buy a brand-new zero-time Stearman biplane.

Prices vary according to your taste, but a top-of-the-line, exquisite MCMD Custom Special, the Rolls-Royce Silver Ghost of Stearman restorations, has a base price of around $30,000 to which must be added the cost of customer options like choice of engine (220, 300, 450 or even a massive 600hp) and instrumentation. MCMD Custom Specials have chrome-plated struts and fittings and 10 coats of hand-rubbed paint. Reade's *pièce de résistance* was a Stearman for the chief pilot of the Gulf Oil Company, resplendent in black and gold, with black leather interior and full dual IFR instrumentation to airline standards. It cost $48,000 in the early 1970s. The Army had paid $9120 for it in 1943. Today it is priceless and the star of the Stearman Restorers Association's annual fly-in at Galesburg, Illinois, set in the rich farmland which the Stearman has helped protect. The old-timers go along and get all dewy-eyed at the sight of long rows of yellow wings again, for few Stearman owners can resist the temptation to paint them in the old 'school' colours.

The Stearman, nearly half a century old, is also the star of many an American airshow, that assault of sight, sound and spectacle which is a triumph of delightful excess, pure theatre, circus and 'razamataz', ill-concealing skills and reflexes tuned to perfect pitch. 'All eyes to center stage now folks' (he means the runway), 'here comes *Ole Smokey*, give him a big hand, let's hear it now' . . . *Ole Smokey* is a Stearman, lacquered in bright red and white checks, its big 450hp Pratt & Whitney going *bloop-bloop-bloop* as it idles past. Atop the upper wing stands a comely young lady (barely) attired in what looks like a Wonder Woman outfit. Pilot Wayne Pierce guns the P & W and the commentator starts his patter, like a Virginia tobacco auctioneer, while *Ole Smokey* lives up to its name and lays a swathe of white across the blue sky:

Wing-riding is nothing new, but with a 450hp Stearman there's so much excess power to counter the drag of the rider that a full aerobatic routine is possible. Loops inside and outside, four-point rolls, slow rolls, eight-point rolls, Cuban eights, stall turns and an ultra-low inverted pass in which you can see the gap between the girl's feet and the centre section as she hangs in the harness with perhaps a yard's clearance between her skull and the runway at 100mph. She is a brave lady, the more so because on ferry flights she had to ride in a windowless compartment right behind the engine firewall where it is hot, smelly and, I imagine, only marginally more comfortable than standing on the wing.

Below: A beautifully restored and maintained example of the most popular of several Stearman Kaydets, a PT-17 finished as an original 'Yellow Peril'.

Bottom: Wayne Pierce and his intrepid 'Wonder Woman' passenger about to start his *Ole Smokey* routine.

GOLDEN AGE: A REVIEW

Left: The Comper Swift was an efficient British single-seat lightplane design between the wars popular for sporting events and fitted with folding wings for economical hangarage. Pictured is one of four Swifts still flying in the UK.

Below: This restored Hawker Tomtit trainer of 1929 vintage was the last of a small number ordered in small batches for the RAF during the between-the-wars years. The Tomtit illustrated, which is regularly flown by the Shuttleworth Trust, was used by Hawker test pilot Alex Henshaw as a hack during World War II, whereafter it was restored by the Hawker company and presented to the Trust.

This Boeing P-12 pursuit
aircraft is a unique
airworthy example of the
between-wars era when
Boeing was an important
builder of fighters. The
F3B/F4B/P-12 series was
introduced in 1928 and
totalled about 600 before
production ended in 1933.
This one is owned by Boeing
and takes to the air on
company occasions and
occasionally at public
airshows.

Far left: A 1918 Nieuport 28 fighter, one of thousands of this French make of World War I scout, preserved in the US, flying over the carrier USS *Antietam* at Pensacola in 1961 on the occasion of the 50th anniversary of the founding of US naval aviation.

Above: The Miles M38 Messenger two-seater was developed during World War II for the British Army for air observation. The Messenger illustrated was bought and restored by Jim Buckingham, finished in the livery of the one used by General Montgomery as his personal liaison aircraft during his Western Desert campaign.

Left: A classic among small pioneering airliners was the de Havilland DH.89A Dragon Rapide, an eight-seater that formed the basis of many an airline's fleet in the 1930s and early post-World War II years. Nearly 750 were built and most were exported. The Rapide illustrated was restored and is owned by the Pioneer Aviation Trust in Jersey, Channel Islands.

Some antique aeroplanes are still employed in profitable service. For example, this Lockheed L10 Electra passenger aircraft, a 10-seater introduced in 1937 as one of a new breed of American airliner, is seen here in service as a jump aircraft for Californian parachutists.

One of a series of widely used and long-lived Grumman flying-boats and amphibians of the 1930s was the J.21 Duck amphibian built for the US Navy and Coast Guard. The one illustrated was retored by Frank Tallman and was one of two used in the film *Murphy's War*.

Previous page: Today it would be an antique aeroplane collector's dream but in 1946, when this photograph of war-surplus Curtiss P-40s close-packed at Walnut Ridge Air Force Base at Arkansas was taken, it was commonplace.

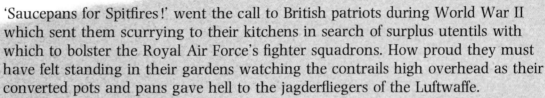

The Hawker Sea Fury, a carrier-borne development of the Fury introduced in 1944, was the last piston-engined fighter of the Fleet Air Arm and entered service after World War II ended, but it was used effectively from British and Australian carriers in the Korean War. The one pictured demonstrating its smoke generators fitted for wingtip Vortex tests is maintained in flying condition by US enthusiast Frank Sanders.

'Saucepans for Spitfires!' went the call to British patriots during World War II which sent them scurrying to their kitchens in search of surplus utentils with which to bolster the Royal Air Force's fighter squadrons. How proud they must have felt standing in their gardens watching the contrails high overhead as their converted pots and pans gave hell to the jagderfliegers of the Luftwaffe.

Sadly, when the war ended Spitfires and many thousands of other warplanes were swiftly converted back to kitchenware without a second thought. Few people realised the extent of the destruction of historic aircraft for two decades. Imagine the surprise of the movie-makers planning *The Battle of Britain* epic who had casually assumed that the Royal Air Force would be able to supply as many airworthy Spitfires, Hurricanes and captured Messerschmitts and Heinkels as they wanted, when they discovered in 1967 that the service could provide only a handful of Spitfires and not a single airworthy Hurricane, much less any German aircraft.

To the film industry must go some of the credit for the revival of interest in flying warbirds which has taken place since then. For *The Battle of Britain*, Group Captain Hamish Mahaddie eventually gathered together a fine collection of elderly warriors — a whole squadron of Spitfires, 50 Spanish-built Heinkel III bombers and 28 Spanish Messerschmitts, many of which have since found their way into the hands of private collectors.

Such was the thoughtless destruction wreaked in breakers' yards in the years following the war that many classic warbirds have disappeared forever; no complete Stirling or Halifax bomber survives, not a Hampden, Blenheim and only one Wellington. British skies have not seen a Beaufighter, Tempest or Typhoon for many long years. German types have suffered even more heavily. At the time of writing there is not one airworthy genuine German-built fighter or bomber to be seen anywhere in the world, although several Messerschmitt Bf 109s and a Focke Wulf Fw 190 are undergoing protracted restoration in the United States, where warplanes have fared better in the care of organisations such as Warbirds of America, the Confederate Air Force (which has a rival, the Damn Yankee Air Force north of the Mason-Dixon line) and the Tallmantz and Planes of Fame Collections in California.

Few private owners can aspire to warbird ownership. Why? Simple economics. Prices of airworthy classic fighter types such as the Spitfire or P-51 Mustang run well into six figures. An engine overhaul may cost £10,000 or more, and if a heavy bomber takes your fancy the cost quadruples. If not actually for millionaires, the more potent and desirable warbirds certainly demand an owner who — as J P Morgan advised potential yacht buyers — can afford not to have to ask the price before buying.

The RAF's most-cherished aeroplane, the Avro Lancaster, after restoration to airworthiness but before acquisition of its dorsal turret.

LANCASTER

There is no sound in the world its equal – four Rolls-Royce Merlins in perfect harmony; and there is just one aeroplane still capable of indulging those whose eyes grow wet when they hear it again – the Avro Lancaster.

The 'Lanc' was the Royal Air Force's most successful heavy bomber of World War II and like many a success it had its beginnings in failure. The Avro Manchester twin-engined bomber designed to a 1936 Air Ministry specification had proved disastrously unreliable, largely because of the dismal performance of its Rolls-Royce Vulture engines which could not develop enough power at altitude and were prone to overheating. Avro's chief designer Roy Chadwick proposed re-engining the bomber with either two Bristol Centaurus or four Rolls-Royce Merlin engines in 1939, but the bureaucrats knew best, and were soon proved wrong when the Manchester simply failed to perform. Chadwick allegedly attended a Ministry-sponsored demonstration of American bombers about this time and stumped off back to his office declaring 'If that's what these idiots think are super bombers, I'll show them!' – and he did.

Taking a Manchester airframe Chadwick designed a new wing to take a four-Merlin in-stallation, for which the Ministry was persuaded to give official blessing in July 1940, and on 13 May the following year the prototype, then known as the Manchester III, made its first flight from Ringway (now Manchester International) Airport. It departed two weeks later for acceptance trials at the Aircraft and Armament Experimental Establishment at Boscombe Down, whose pilots declared it eminently suitable for operational service. Production of the renamed Lancaster began in 1942 at five factories whose monthly output rose to over 300 aircraft.

The Manchester/Merlin combination proved an inspired union which ran to 7366 aircraft. Lancasters flew 156,000 sorties during the war, eventually equipped 56 Bomber Command squadrons, and dropped 608,612 tons of bombs, including 12,000lb 'Tallboy' and 22,000lb 'Grand Slam earthquake' bombs, and Sir Barnes Wallis's famous mine, or 'bouncing bomb', immortalised by 617 'Dambusters' Squadron. Although nearly half the total number of Lancasters produced were lost in action the aeroplane was regarded as one of the safest bombers, inasmuch as *any* bomber can truly be called safe. In the first year of Lancaster raids 152 tons of bombs were dropped for every aeroplane lost, three times better than the Stirling, and two dozen Lancasters managed to clock up 100 missions apiece, which was almost akin to immortality among bombers and popularly (if

wrongly) supposed to bring continued good fortune to all who flew in them.

The Lancaster was a 'pussycat' to fly, 'like a four-engined Tiger Moth' it was said, although the Moth is not nearly so pleasant to handle as nostalgia would have it. The 'Lanc''s greenhouse canopy, worthy of Kew Gardens, offered splendid visibility, though when the flak was thickest one would have been glad not to have had such a fine viewpoint.

However sweet its handling, a Lancaster cannot have been a pleasant place in which to die in the dark above Germany where an unseen night-fighter pilot could hit the 'Lanc''s jugular vein – the fuel cells in the wings – while the bomber's three gunners strained desperately to get a sight of him in the blackness. Once free of the enemy coast and out of range of fighters they would relax a little, think of bacon and eggs for breakfast, and perhaps of the pestering desk-

Here *City of Lincoln*, flagship of the Battle of Britain Memorial Flight, completes a typical low pass during one of its closely scheduled appearances at airshows around the UK.

fliers who would want their tiresome paperwork done, probably in triplicate, before they could sleep. This ditty sung to the tune of 'The Church's One Foundation' captures the spirit of the bomber boys to perfection.

> *We are the heavy bombers, we try to do out bit,*
> *We fly through concentrations of flak with sky all lit,*
> *And when we drop our cargoes, we do not give a damn,*
> *The eggs may miss the goods yard, but they muck up poor old Hamm.*
>
> *And when in adverse weather the winds are all to hell,*
> *The navigator's balled up, the wireless balled as well,*
> *We think of all the popsies we've known in days gone by,*
> *And curse the silly beggars who taught us how to fly.*
>
> *And in the Heavenly Ops Room, St Peter will enquire.*
> *'Did you cause an explosion or start a damn great fire?'*
> *But when you see the angels tapping faultless morse,*
> *You realise your QDM was a reciprocal course,*
>
> *And if you go to Hades it's just like SHQ,*
> *There's lots of stooges sitting round with damn-all else to do.*
> *They ask you for your flimsies, your pass and target maps,*
> *And you take the ruddy issue and stuff it down their traps.*

The Royal Air Force is custodian of the sole airworthy Lancaster, although two Canadian-built examples, one with the Strathallan Collection in Scotland, the other with the Canadian Warplanes Heritage Group of Hamilton, Ontario, are being groomed to fly again.

The RAF's last flying 'Lanc', *City of Lincoln*, is the flagship of the Battle of Britain Memorial Flight, curiously perhaps, for the Lancaster was still on Roy Chadwick's drawing board in the summer of 1940. This particular machine was built in 1945 and served as a photo-reconnaissance aircraft in the Far East, Middle East and Africa, ending its operational days as a flying laboratory at the Royal Aircraft Establishment at Cranfield, Bedfordshire, before being placed on 'guard duty' at RAF Waddington.

The arrival of a privately owned airworthy Lancaster from Australia either inspired or shamed the RAF into getting their last 'Lanc' into the air again (ironically the privately owned machine is now a gate guardian at RAF Scampton, home of the 'Dambusters' 617 Squadron which now flies another Avro aeroplane, the Vulcan bomber), and *City of Lincoln* is now perhaps the Service's most cherished aeroplane. For years it flew devoid of the distinctive mid-upper turret until a globetrotting businessman spotted just such an object in Argentina and the Royal Navy, quick to help the 'junior service,' shipped it home.

Lancaster *City of Lincoln* now lives at RAF Coningsby in Lincolnshire, whose people got together a 20,000-signature petition pleading for the return of Britain's most famous bomber to the county from which so many set forth on the great raids of World War II. She flies just 65 meticulously counted hours each year, flown by Squadron Leader K R 'Jacko' Jackson whose enviable duty it is to be the aeroplane's only full-time crew member. His task is a rewarding one, not just for the pleasure of flying the Lancaster, but from the pleasure the sight and sound of it gives to spectators at airshows – in 1977 'Jacko' Jackson flew *City of Lincoln* low over the Derwent valley reservoir to commemorate the Dambusters raid in front of survivors of the original mission.

B-17 FLYING FORTRESS

. . . The waiting was the worst. You would get used to being roused from fitful sleep long chilly hours before daybreak by flashlight-waving mess orderlies. Sometimes you might even enjoy the three-in-the-morning breakfast of coffee, canned peaches, bread with apple butter, pancakes and stomach-turning dehydrated egg. But the *waiting*! Those anxious bleary-eyed moments at briefing, where anticipation lay as heavy as the cigarette smoke as you tried to guess today's target. Ludwigshafen, the grapevine said. Or Frankfurt. Or Magdeburg. Or Politz again, where 50 of your buddies went missing last week. Or maybe even the worst of all, Big B – Berlin itself. Riding the jeep out to the flightline in the early morning East Anglian mist you would disguise your fear and war-weariness in exaggerated camaraderie and self-conscious humour, sweating out the interminable minutes to take-off time thinking, praying, and performing personal little rituals to ward off the gremlins and the Luftwaffe.

But today there is no sinister covered-up map of *Festung Europa* on the briefing-room wall. The only German fighters we will see are a pair of friendly F-104 Starfighters parked beside us; the only 'flak' will come from airshow control if we overrun our allotted time-slot. We are time-travellers, weekend warriors riding back 35 years on the 'Big Ass Bird' — a B-17G Flying Fortress in the markings of the United States Eighth Air Force, complete with obligatory reclining nude on the nose and the broad blue diagonal fin stripe of the 457th Bombardment Group, the *Fireball Outfit*, which operated from Glatton near Peterborough. *Sally B* is one of the last of 12,751 Fortresses built, and one of just a handful still flying. She was completed too late for combat and served in USAF training commands and as a high-altitude photo-mapping aircraft with France's Institut Geographique National before joining the USAAF Memorial Flight run by Englishman Don Bullock from the former Royal Air Force and USAAF base at Duxford near Cambridge. One other Fortress is flying in Europe; several still earn their livings as fire-bombers in the United States and carrying cargo in South America, and a few — like *Sally B* — have been restored to their wartime colours for display flying.

Early Flying Fortresses scarcely lived up to the

named first coined by a *Seattle Daily Times* caption writer. They were woefully under-armed, vulnerable to frontal attack and had nasty reputations as 'flamers' when hit. Reichsmarschall Göring called them 'flying coffins' and 'Bomber' Harris remarked tartly that their armament would be more appropriately located in an amusement park than in a war aeroplane'. Not so the B-17G, which was the most heavily armed and best defended Fortress of all; there were 13 .50-calibre Browning M-2 machine guns, two in each tail 'stinger', upper, ball and remotely operated chin turrets, one apiece at the waist hatches, nose cheeks and radio operator's station, each with 500–700 rounds of ammunition, five armour-piercing to one of tracer.

Come for a ride in this flying legend, this symbol of American air power. Swing up inelegantly through the rear door and crawl back past the tailwheel housing to the 'Cheyenne' tail turret, where you squatted on your knees, legs doubled up beneath you, for hour after numbing hour. Yours was the big bomber's most important defensive position, though it brought you little comfort, for it was also the one which enemy fighters invariably went for first.

Sally B's Brownings have long gone, her turrets faired over with aluminium panels, but the plexiglas which filled the waist hatches now

A wartime picture of a B-17 Flying Fortress, contrails streaming, with bomb-bay doors open and bombs ready to go.

makes fine panoramic windows. On earlier Fortresses one had to slide the panels open and fire her guns in the 40-below blast of 'hurricane alley', swaddled in silk socks and inner gloves, woollen combinations, electrically heated suit, flak-jacket, fleece-lined trousers, jacket, gloves and boots and a tight-fitting oxygen mask which itched miserably if you left any stubble when you shaved and felt like a dog muzzle.

If you were the crew's little guy you would be ball-gunner, hunched embryo-like below the aeroplane's belly in a fishbowl turret whose vulnerable appearance belied the paradox that it was statistically the safest crew position in combat. You sighted your twin Brownings between your feet and fired them with arms arched sharply above your head. When things got busy

Two pictures of the Duxford-based Fortress, *Sally B*, (left) on a Duxford airshow day and making a low pass over Shoreham, Sussex, Airport during a flying display.

the guns glowed red and spent ammunition links piled high in the bottom of the turret faster than you could shovel them out of the chute.

Ahead of the ball turret *Sally B*'s radio room has been replaced by a row of passenger seats. As radioman you sat in the dark centre fuselage with just a porthole out of which to catch a glimpse of the action if you were not too busy. Your primary function was to sit at your set receiving messages from base or divisional headquarters which you decoded from a ricepaper key-for-the-day. If there was a chance of going down you ate it.

You would take navigational fixes from radio beacons; transmit half-hourly position reports at prearranged co-ordinates to enable your 'little friends' – the P-51 and P-47 escort fighters – to rendezvous with the formation; keep the pilot-controlled liaison and command sets properly tuned; and work the IFF (identify friend or foe) equipment. You were also the crew's first-aid man whose job it was to patch the wounded and comfort the dying, and it was also your unenviable job to balance like a high-wire walker on the narrow catwalk over the open bomb-bay and

trip free any bombs which had hung up on their racks, and to switch on the big K-24 strike cameras which fired every 10 seconds over the target, recording not only the destruction of the enemy but often of your own kind as well — haunting obscene images of broken wrenched-apart Fortresses fluttering away like silver sycamores, or disappearing in brief vicious flashes of high explosive, petrol, oxygen and human flesh; 30 tons of aeroplane and 10 men gone in a shutter's blink.

Take care across the catwalk as we edge through the plywood cockpit door. Outside the ground crew are busily pulling through the four 12-foot diameter Hamilton Standard propellers of the Wright Cyclone GR-1820-97 radial engines, which develop 1200hp each at take-off and are good for 1380hp at altitude thanks to their General Electric B-22 exhaust-driven turbochargers.

The crew chief gives a thumbs-up gesture, points to the number three engine and circles a finger in the air. The Cyclone coughs, catches and pumps out great gouts of grey smoke which swirl off in the propwash like oily contrails. Soon all four are turning and *Sally B* shakes and shudders to the Cyclone quartet's vibrant tune. Away go the chocks and we move off to the accompaniment of a Spike Jones cacophony of throbbing radials and squealing brakes, Don Bullock steering with blasts of differential throttle on the outer engines, a task made easier by the Fortress's throttles which are shaped like a letter F and arranged so that the middle segments come together to form a common grip.

Going off on a mission you were glad of that as you took your place in the swaying lumbering conga-line heading for the runway. From behind, the Fortresses looked like hump-backed eagles, their olive-drabness relieved by colourful splashes of individuality to which the Air Force top brass usually turned a blind eye. The thinly disguised double entendres with which you christened your bombers sometimes upset the folks back home, though. *Jamaica ?*, *Virgin-on-the-Verge*, *Heavenly Body*, and *Grin-an-Bare-It* were favourites, though some went for macho names like *E-rat-icator*, *Knockout Dropper*, or *Murder Inc.*, and there was always an optimistic *Flak Dodger*. A good squadron artist could earn $15 a time for painting a copy of one of Alberto Vargas's dream-perfect *Esquire* girls on the nose of a 'Fort'. Occasionally Air Force Command would try to censor your efforts, and you would have the artist apply a tasteful swimsuit in water-soluble paint for inspection time. It always rained in England.

Today we are alone at the runway holding point, stifling in the hot cockpit. The tower gives a green light and Bullock walks the four throttles forward to a raucous reverberating 45 inches of manifold pressure before handing the engines over to co-pilot Keith Sissons while he puts both hands on the half-moon shaped control wheel. The pounding of the four Cyclones is as startling as a disco to a maiden aunt, though the acceleration seems ponderous and we roll for an age before lifting off at 90mph. Surely nothing this big, this heavy, can be made to fly at 90mph?

We have barely climbed to 300 feet when Bullock pulls back the power and rolls hard left, banking 60 degrees until *Sally B* flies wingtip-to-wingtip with her own shadow undulating across the grass. This is no way to treat an old bomber, but now we are almost at ground level again, running in along the crowd line then zooming in a steep climbing turn, *g* forces pushing us hard into the cushionless metal seats. The Fortress is astonishingly manoeuvrable (they were looped and spun during the war, not always intentionally), but it is heavy on the controls and Don Bullock has to work hard to keep *Sally B* tightly within the airfield boundary as we nose down again and come in so low that the view from the cockpit looks just as it did when we were parked on the ramp. Landing lights ablaze, we roar on past the crowd to be applauded by the clicks of a thousand cameras.

It must have been like this when you had finished your 25-mission tour of duty. Elated at having survived you would do a good buzz job back at base, or better still at someone else's base, and hope that the tower controllers would understand as you swerved at the very last second to avoid them and that they would record your little indiscretion as a beat-up by an un-identified 'Fort', even though they could read your tail number and unit marking with only half an eye. Buzzing was a grounding offence if you were caught, but what the hell? And if you came across one of your arch-rivals, a B-24 Liberator, you would creep up behind and go sailing past with your waist gunners making rude signs through their open hatches.

Back on the ground after a mission measured in minutes rather than hours we climb down, perspiration-soaked, and sit beneath *Sally B*'s wings drinking cold beers and listening to the metallic pings of her cooling engines. She costs a small fortune to maintain and fly, but there is no more fitting tribute to the 79,000 American airmen who died over Europe during World War II, and we raise our beers in salute.

MOSQUITO

Geoffrey de Havilland's idea seemed logical enough; like Ernst Heinkel before him, he planned to build a lightweight bomber able to outfly enemy fighters but, unlike the German, de Havilland's aeroplane would have the advantage of the best engines in the world. Off to the Air Ministry he went in 1937 to outline his project to the desk-bound mandarins, feeling not a little smug one imagines. The men at the ministry were not pleased. 'Forget it,' they told him, 'No one builds aeroplanes from wood any more, and besides, you know nothing about military aeroplanes.' They suggested that de Havilland might perhaps help out with some small job, designing a wing for a new Ministry project called the Ape, perhaps?

Resigned to ministerial myopia, de Havilland proceeded in secret with his bomber, working at an old country mansion named Salisbury Hall about five miles from the company factory at Hatfield in Hertfordshire. Drawing on the company's experience with the all-wood Comet-racer and Albatross airliner, a revolutionary structure was devised comprising inner and outer fuselage skins of plywood with balsa-wood infilling which resulted in a light yet stiff airframe requiring no additional structure. Better still, the fuselage could be built in two separate halves, much like a modern plastic model aeroplane kit, and joined after all internal equipment, wiring and control runs had been installed, thus greatly reducing manufacturing time.

The prototype de Havilland DH.98 Mosquito was built in a farmyard of Salisbury Hall (now a museum dedicated to the aeroplane and featuring that first 'Mossie') and made its first flight on 25 November 1940, by which time the Whitehall bureaucrats had relented and sanctioned its development. Geoffrey de Havilland Junior made the first test flight. 'I was certain that we had in the Mosquito a real war-winning plane,' his father wrote in his autobiography, *Sky Fever*

One of an early Leavesden-built batch of DH Mosquitos, restored to flying condition by the manufacturer making almost a touch-and-go low pass as it adds to the variety of a Shuttleworth Trust flying day at Old Warden.

The restored Mosquito showing off its elegant lines to best advantage during the visit to Old Warden.

(Hamish Hamilton, London 1961), 'but this did not prevent me from fretting about the multitude of things that could go wrong. I was, after all, about to be the spectator of what I suspected was to be the most momentous take-off of any of our planes.'

How right he was. But nothing did go wrong on that first trial, and the Mosquito's creators were themselves astonished at its speed and manoeuvrability, even on one engine. Within three months the 'Wooden Wonder' was firmly established as the world's fastest operational aircraft, and so versatile did it promise to be that plans were soon in hand to adapt it to wide-ranging roles – fighter, photo-reconnaissance, night intruder, pathfinder, even high-speed courier.

It was the photo-recce Mosquito which first entered service with the Royal Air Force, making its debut on 20 September 1941 when a Mosquito Mark I flew over Brest, La Pallice, Bordeaux and Paris in daylight at 23,000 feet and easily left behind would-be intercepting Messerschmitt Bf 109s. The Mosquito's speed was astonishing. With twice the weight of a Spitfire (and twice the power, admittedly), it could outpace the fighters and with one propeller feathered could hold its own against a Hurricane.

As a bomber the Mosquito could carry up to a 4000lb bombload all the way to Berlin at almost twice the speed of the American B-17, which initially carried little more load and needed a 10-man crew. The first bomber Mosquitos entered RAF service in May 1942 amid great excitement, for here was a bomber that behaved like a fighter,

that was for two and half years to be the fastest warplane of any kind in the world, and one that was to play a vital part in the winning of the war.

The Mosquito's existence was not publicly announced until September 1942 when four Mark IV bombers attacked the Gestapo head-quarters in the centre of Oslo in the daring low-level raid which was to become the *modus operandi* of so many Mosquito missions, nipping in like its namesake, biting quickly and flying away. Reichsmarschall Göring himself fell victim to the 'Mossie' on 31 January 1943 when a bombing mission to Berlin by Mosquitos from 105 Squadron was perfectly timed to wreck a parade which he was addressing. Göring raged. 'I turn green and yellow with envy when I see a Mosquito,' he ranted, 'the British knock together a beautiful wooden aircraft that every piano factory over there is building. . . . There is nothing the British do not have.'

Indeed it must have seemed like that, for the Mosquitos flew fast and high, unarmed and unafraid their two-man crews metaphorically if not literally thumbing their noses at the Luft-waffe. Most fascinating of all the Mosquito operations was the 'airline' service run by British Overseas Airways Corporation between Britain and Nazi-marooned Sweden. Swedish neutrality (in name if not in deed) permitted British aircraft to land on her soil, and Sweden was a valuable source of the ball bearings vital to British in-dustry. Thus Mosquitos were hastily painted in civilian markings and began a high-speed shuttle service between Leuchars in Scotland and Stock-holm in Sweden on what came to be known as the 'ball-bearing airline'.

Flown by civilian crews the Mosquitos raced full throttle, the exhaust stacks of their Merlin engines glowing red against the night skies, their bomb bays filled with agents, diplomatic pouches, mail and newspapers on the outward journey, ball bearings on the way back. It was an excruciatingly hazardous occupation, made possible only by the speed of the Mosquito and its agility as an aerial escapologist. In three years of operations, some of which saw a dozen aircraft on the route at the same time, only four Mosquitos and 10 people were lost. As if further tribute to the 'Mossie's' fleetness of wing was needed, it is worth recording that some Mosquito bombers totalled more than 200 missions apiece, a record unequalled by any other Allied bomber of the war.

Few Mosquito crews would argue with the Air Marshal who declared it the finest aeroplane ever built, for de Havilland's designers had found the perfect combination of airframe and engine resulting in an unrivalled power-to-weight ratio and an aeroplane which was readily adaptable to a multitude of unforeseen roles. It was not, however, an easy aeroplane to fly. The immense power of the two Merlins came as a rude awakening to tyro fliers used to the docile Airspeed Oxford trainers on which they did their multi-engine conversion courses. Letting the engine torque get the better of you on take-off led to an immediate and dangerous swing, and while the Mosquito performed engine-out better than some contemporaries did with both running, loss of an engine at take-off was especially critical in a 'Mossie' because the minimum engine-out control speed (that is the lowest speed at which there is sufficient rudder power available to counteract the asymmetric thrust) was about 80 knots higher than the speed at which it lifted off – a lethal situation if an engine failed before the aircraft had accelerated through the critical speed.

Such is the affection for the Mosquito that its manufacturers, whose revered name is now lost forever among the faceless nationalised conglomerate called British Aerospace, still retains one for demonstration purposes, and two more of the total of 7781 built are still flying in England – one with the Strathallan Collection — as tributes to the days when wooden wings and nerves of steel took over from Sir Francis Drake's wooden walls and hearts of oak in the defence of England.

FAIREY SWORDFISH

Picture this scene. His Majesty's aircraft carrier *Illustrious* sailing up the English Channel in 1940. On the bridge an American naval officer seconded to the British Fleet Air Arm stares in disbelief at the Fairey Swordfish torpedo-bombers ranged on her deck. 'My God!', he exclaims, 'You don't mean to say that you *fly* those things? They look more like four-poster bedsteads than front-line airplanes!'

He was right. Open-cockpit fabric-and-wire

The Fleet Air Arm Historic Flight's Swordfish on a typical airshow demonstration flight.

Observer/gunner's view from the rear cockpit of a Swordfish.

oil rig. Empty, the 'Stringbag' weighs 4700lb; in service it was frequently operated at an overload gross almost double that. You climb *up*, rather than into, the Swordfish, scaling its fuselage sides with the help of spring-loaded toe-holds which snap at your boots as you go. The pilot sits high up on a hump, and can see forwards both over and under the wing centre section, while observer and air-gunner occupy a dugout-like pit behind, which has no seats, so you must either squat down on your parachute pack or stand.

The 750hp Pegasus nine-cylinder radial engine – the 'Stringbag' pilot's beloved, reliable 'Peggy' – has an inertia starter with a heavy flywheel which must be energised with a plug-in handcrank. It is hard exhausting labour for the ground engineer. Cheeks puffed, face purple, he cranks ever more quickly, as if winding up an enormous clockwork toy. It takes two minutes of arm-jellifying cranking to get 'Peggy' firing. What must it have been like on the pitching deck of a carrier at sea?

Take-off power brings the Swordfish's tail up immediately and it lifts off at about 45 knots. From a carrier's deck in strong winds the Swordfish would be airborne as soon as the throttle was opened, and some aircraft flying from MACships (merchant aircraft carriers) even had rocket-assisted take-off tubes for helicopter-like ascents from their short decks.

Low-speed manoeuvrability and excellent control response were always the 'Stringbag''s strongpoints. Though slow and sedate, it was capable of the tightest of manoeuvres at wave-top height in perfect safety, making the lumbering biplanes no easy targets for attacking fighters or shore-based guns. During the Norwegian campaign Swordfish crews would fly low right up against the sides of fjords, luring Luftwaffe Messerschmitts into narrow valleys from which the faster less-manoeuvrable fighters were unable to escape; some were destroyed without the Swordfish gunners firing a shot.

Standing up in an aeroplane whose fuselage sides barely reach your waist gives you a rude awakening to the malevolence of the elements. Imagine the discomforts of the men who flew far out over the grey Atlantic, from small merchant ships whose living quarters were as cramped as the Swordfish's cockpit; or of those who ranged out over the Arctic Circle where raw winds savaged crews who – through administrative blunders – were never issued with the fleece-lined flying suits which their colleagues, snug in heated closed cockpits, had.

Exhausted by endless hours of duty, stiff and

biplanes must have seemed eccentric indeed to a man accustomed to the US Navy's TBDs and TBMs. The Swordfish was an anachronism, dating from 1932, yet it served throughout World War II, outlasted its intended replacement, and sank a greater tonnage of enemy shipping than any other Allied aircraft. Its forte lay in its load-carrying ability – torpedoes, bombs, rockets, mines – for which it earned the affectionate nickname 'Stringbag' when someone observed that 'no housewife on a shopping spree could cram a wider variety of articles into her stringbag'.

Originally known as the Fairey TSR-2 (for torpedo-spotter-reconnaissance), the Swordfish first flew from Great West Aerodrome, on the site of London Heathrow Airport, on 21 March 1933. A total of 2391 was built, virtually all wartime production coming from Blackburn Aircraft's plant at Sherburn-in-Elmet, while Fairey devoted its factory to Albacores, which Blackburn also built. The Swordfish was thus one of very few aeroplanes ever to have been in series production right alongside its successor. Even the DC-3 never managed that.

Only one Swordfish survives today in airworthy condition, the pride of the Royal Navy's Historic Aircraft Flight based at the Fleet Air Arm Museum at Yeovilton in Somerset. It is a mammoth biplane, standing high up on undercarriage legs which look as if they might support a small

Below: Swordfish close-up illustrating the steep climb using flapped toe-holds needed to reach the cockpit.

Bottom: Less elegant perhaps, but still looking 'right' in its own functional way, is this RN Historic Aircraft Flight's Swordfish.

numb from the merciless cold, the pilots would sometimes fall asleep at the controls, to be woken by blows from their observers, whose tiny cubicles, cluttered with parachute, charts, chartboard, protractors, dividers, course-and-speed calculator, Wilkinson Computer, pencils and erasers, were not conducive to peaceful slumber. With frozen fingers they struggled to make drift sightings through a perspex window in the floor, or fought the slipstream to take compass bearings, dead-reckoning across tens of thousands of square miles of featureless and unfriendly ocean, often in darkness to find the way back to the speck of floating steel which was home.

Worst off were crews flying from merchant convoys, for the Swordfish — a heavy, underpowered monument to high drag — was an inveterate sluggard whose supposed maximum speed of 125 knots was highly optimistic, and could be reduced almost to zero by strong headwinds. A sudden change in wind direction while the Swordfish was patrolling astern of the convoy could mean a struggling return, with the gale reducing groundspeed to a crawl and the possibility of U-boat attack preventing the ships from stopping to wait for the aircraft. On occasions the Swordfish had to ditch, fuel exhausted in the futile chase, with scarcely a hope of rescue.

Ponderous performance could sometimes be turned to advantage. When approaching a rolling sea-swamped carrier deck pitching as high as a house, instant controllability at 55 knots or less was a fine thing to have. The relative movement between biplane and deck could often be but a few knots and the landing consequently gossamer-soft in contrast to the bone-jarring arrivals of heavier aircraft which had literally to be flown onto the deck. It was not uncommon for a loosely picketed Swordfish to become airborne in Atlantic gales, hovering in flying attitude just above the deck, but with power off this heavy

biplane had all the grace of a lead balloon and an engine failure, thankfully rare, meant a very prompt return to earth. (Cross-country trips in the Royal Navy's treasured Swordfish are planned to avoid inhospitable terrain and, ironically in view of its record, flight over open water is forbidden.)

For shipping attacks you could push over into a near-vertical dive from 10,000 feet, secure in the knowledge that the airspeed would never rise above 200 knots thanks to the drag-ridden airframe, and that you could safely hold your dive to within a couple of hundred feet of the water, drooping all four ailerons to act as dive-brakes if necessary (though this facility was rarely used in service). The success of the 'Stringbag' in such strikes can scarcely have done much for the morale of enemy admirals who saw the prides of their fleets sunk or crippled by rickety birdcage biplanes.

Narvik, Bomba Bay, Cape Matapan, Taranto, North Atlantic, the sinking of the *Bismarck*, campaigns in the Mediterranean and Western Desert — the Swordfish's battle honours are legendary. Its role as a torpedo-bomber ended in 1942 with the catastrophic attempt to prevent the breakout of the German battleships *Gneisenau*, *Prinz Eugen* and *Scharnhorst* from Brest Harbour. Six of the ancient biplanes, led by Lieutenant-Commander Eugene 'Winkle' Esmonde, were pulverised by the ships' guns in the attack, for which the brave Esmonde was posthumously awarded the Victoria Cross.

Thereafter the Swordfish performed its greatest work as a reconnaissance spotter, coastal-patrol bomber, minelayer and submarine hunter-killer. In action from the outset, it was, appropriately, a Swordfish which flew the last British operation of the war in Europe, against a midget submarine in the English Channel just four hours before the German surrender.

The Swordfish inspired in those who flew it (and many who did not) a fierce undying loyalty, remembered each year on Taranto Night when survivors of the raid gather at Fleet Air Arm headquarters at Lee-on-Solent in Hampshire to toast again their beloved 'Stringbag'. What is its charisma? Not good looks, not speed, nor comfort, for sure. Sweet-handling vicelessness is part of it, but mostly it is old-fashioned dependability, an aeroplane to which men willingly entrusted their lives and went to war confident that, whatever else, the 'Stringbag' would never let them down, would take all the punishment that they could administer, and then would bring them home safely again. A friendly aeroplane.

FIESELER STORCH

Berlin, 26 April 1945, is a city cut off by the advances of American, British and Russian forces. Adolf Hitler waits in his secret bunker amid the ruins of his 'Thousand Year Reich' which has lasted just 12 infamous years. He has summoned General Ritter von Greim to his presence, so that he can promote him to command the Luftwaffe in place of the discredited Hermann Göring. There is no way into the beleaguered capital . . . except one. Low over the smouldering ruins of the city comes an ugly stick-insect of an aeroplane, flying at treetop level. At the controls is von Greim; behind him stands the Führer's personal pilot, Flugkapitan Hanna Reitsch, ready to take over if the General is hit. And he is, by Russian small arms fire. She grabs stick and throttle, still leaning over the wounded von Greim, and flies the aeroplane right into the heart of Berlin, landing on Unter den Linden.

The vehicle of this incredible, if futile, piece of bravado was a Fieseler Storch, an aeroplane which first appeared in the late spring of 1936 to meet a Luftwaffe requirement for an army co-operation, casualty evacuation and liaison aircraft. Reinhold Mewes, chief designer for Gerhard Fieseler, opted for a high-wing monoplane of conventional construction, but employed advanced STOL (short take-off and landing) techniques to provide unrivalled slow-speed flight. So successful was the Storch at operating from confined spaces that within a year of its appearance the Reichsluftfahrtministerium (German Aviation Ministry) ordered work on autogiros to be halted; the Storch could do all that rotary winged craft could do, and more.

But even von Greim's unorthodox arrival in Berlin was a mere humdrum commuter trip compared to the rescue of Italian dictator Benito Mussolini from incarceration on a peak of the Gran Sasso Massif in 1943. Il Duce, out of favour with the Italian regime, had been interned in the Hotel Rifugio at Abruzzi, more than 9000 feet up and accessible only by cable car. On 12 September 1943 Hitler dispatched a force of 12 gliders to land Wehrmacht troops on the rock-strewn mountainside. The gliders crashed to the ground, for there was barely a clear patch anywhere, certainly not enough on which to land, and waited for the arrival of the Focke-Achgelis Fa-223 helicopter which was to pluck Mussolini to safety. It never came, having become unserviceable at the last moment. SS Hauptsturmführer

Otto Skorzeny, who led the expedition, took a gamble; he ordered the Storch spotter aircraft circling overhead to pick up the Italian dictator. Incredibly it worked. The Storch landed on a two-hundred-foot strip of rocky mountainside, collected the terrified Mussolini, and plucked him from one of the most impenetrable spots on earth.

The Storch's routine service was much less glamorous. They served as rugged aerial jeeps in every theatre of the war, and were built in Germany, Czechoslovakia and France, where the Morane Saulnier company continued production in peacetime as the MS 500/501/502 Criquet series.

Most surviving airworthy Storches (2549 were built) are French Moranes, identifiable by their all-metal wings in place of the wooden surfaces on Fieseler-built aircraft. Apparently patriotic French workers at the Morane factories were given to sabotaging Storches by urinating into the glue used to assemble the wings, hence the change to metal.

One such Morane is owned by the Honourable Patrick Lindsay, an English collector of antique aeroplanes and vintage cars who has had his Morane MS 500 restored in full Luftwaffe camouflage. Lindsay is in good company; during the war Lord Montgomery of Alamein used a personal Storch during the Western Desert campaign, while Prime Minister Winston Churchill toured the Normandy beaches in another captured machine in 1944.

The Storch is an absurd looking machine, a caricature of an aeroplane, like an enormous science fiction praying mantis creature. It sits on stilty long-stroke undercarriage legs which enable it to take off and land at extreme angles of attack, so tall that even a six-footer can barely peer over the sills of its multi-faceted cockpit. The cabin is a maze of flat glass panels which offer 360-degree visibility; the side panels are canted outwards so that you can look straight down. Huge 48-foot planks of wings are festooned with full-length leading-edge slots and flaps which automatically droop the ailerons when lowered and increase the wing area by 18 percent. They are operated by a bicycle-chain system which clanks uncomfortably close to the pilot's left ear, but they are mightily effective. The Storch will lift off at barely 35mph after a ground run of as little as 50 yards — five times its own length — and can be made to hover with zero groundspeed in a

This picture of the UK Wycombe Air Park Storch gives it more of a dragonfly appearance, but the frail-looking spars and struts were designed for and stood up to rough-field take-off and landing.

25-knot wind or even travel backwards when it blows hard. Into wind the Storch can be landed nearly vertically, those long legs dangling like a cranefly's to absorb the impact. Luftwaffe pilots were cautioned against using the fierce brakes on landing lest they snatch and shear off the spindly undercarriage.

Though it does amazing things the Storch is not easy to fly. It has little natural stability and needs to be flown all the time; definitely not a 'hands off' machine, for its controls are poorly harmonised, heavy and sluggish and while it can keep flying at speeds below 30mph, its stall when it comes produces excursions in pitch and roll which divided Luftwaffe Storch fliers into two categories — the quick and the dead. Slow (it cruises at 80mph on a 240hp Argus AS10C inverted V-8 engine), ungainly, gawky and ugly, the Storch had few friends among those who flew her, and a legion of admirers among those who —

like Benito Mussolini — were plucked to safety from inaccessible spots no bigger than table napkins.

GRUMMAN WILDCAT HELLCAT/BEARCAT

The Grumman factory on Long Island is known to everyone in aviation as the 'Iron Works' because of its reputation for producing rugged nearly indestructible aeroplanes. During its first five years in business Leroy Grumman's company built a series of innovative fighter biplanes for the US Navy, commencing with the FF-1 'Fifi' which was the first American naval aeroplane to have a retractable undercarriage. The biplane series progressed through the F3F 'flying barrel' which was in flight test when design work began in November 1935 on a high-performance suc-

Oldest of the famous Grumman 'cat' family is the Wildcat, here represented by an immaculate example based with the Confederate Air Force.

cessor, the XF4F-1.

The story goes that one day in the summer of 1936 designer Dick Hutton and engineer Bill Schwendler were poring over their latest biplane drawings when Hutton reached over and drew an aerofoil section at the fuselage centreline, converting biplane to monoplane in a stroke.

Grumman test pilot Bob Hall made the new monoplane XF4F-2's first flight on 2 September 1937 and just before Christmas that year the aircraft was delivered to the naval test center at Anacostia, Virginia, for a fly-off competition against the Seversky NF-1 and Brewster XF2A-1. Disaster compounded disaster. The aircraft caught fire in the air, engine bearings failed, the deck arrester hook broke, and finally the Grumman crashed after its 1050hp Pratt & Whitney Twin Wasp engine failed. The Navy decided they liked the Brewster design better, though as events turned out it was the wrong decision, for the Buffalo was a dismal aeroplane which some squadron commanders are rumoured to have wrecked deliberately so that they could get Grumman replacements.

Undeterred, the Grumman team persevered with a redesign of the aircraft and their gamble paid off; on 8 August 1939 the US Navy ordered 78 production F4F-3s and export orders came in from France and Greece, though in both cases the aircraft were diverted to the British Fleet Air Arm, who called them Martlets. It was not until the autumn of 1941 that the US Navy adopted the name Wildcat for the stubby little fighter, thus inaugurating a long battle-honoured line

Pictured at the US Navy Museum, Pensacola, is the biplane forerunner of Grumman's famous family of cats, the FF-1, 'Fifi'; it had the USN's first retractable undercarriage 'inherited' by Grumman from earlier Loening central-float amphibians.

of Grumman 'cats', continued to the present F-14 Tomcat swing-wing carrier fighter.

The Wildcat was the only modern fighter on the US Navy inventory at the time of Pearl Harbor, and while it was inferior in many respects to its principal adversary, the Mitsubishi Zero, the Wildcat could absorb tremendous punishment. One US Marine Corps pilot claimed that a Wildcat could take 15 minutes continuous fire from a Zero and survive; a two-second burst from the Grumman's four .50 machine guns was usually enough to bring down the lighter Japanese fighter, which had no self-sealing fuel tanks or armour-plating.

The Wildcat had one quirk which did not endear it to its pilots; the distinctive 'knock-kneed' undercarriage which it inherited from the earlier Grumman biplanes was retracted by turning a hand crank in the cockpit. You could always identify a newcomer to the aeroplane by his weaving flight pattern after take-off when the cranking motion (it took 29 turns) was transmitted through his body to the stick. And if you had the misfortune to let the handle slip through your fingers before the wheels retracted it unwound wildly and would break your wrist if you tried to catch it. The Wildcat's narrow roller-skate-like undercarriage also made it tricky to handle on the ground. Arrester wires took care of the problem at sea, but pilots coming ashore after carrier duty were guaranteed to amuse bystanders with the occasional ground-loop.

Wildcat production continued until the war's end, but long before that, in 1941, Grumman began assessing the first combat reports from F4F pilots and projected a new larger and faster fighter designated XF6F-1, for which the US Navy placed a prototype order on 30 June that year. The aircraft was redesignated XF6F-3 early in development, and the first production aeroplane was completed barely 15 months after the award of the initial prototype contract. Powered by a 2000hp Pratt & Whitney R2800 Double Wasp, the F6F-3 Hellcat was armed with six .50 Brownings in the outer wing panels. Gone was all that hand-cranking; the Hellcat's undercarriage rotated 90 degrees then folded flat into the wings.

It was a formidable aeroplane. Grumman's designers and engineers had learned the lessons of the Wildcat's weaknesses against the Zero well. In particular the Hellcat lived up to the 'Iron Works' title, for engineer Bill Schwendler doubled or trebled every design safety margin quoted in the US Navy specification (this was known around the works as the 'Schwendler Factor'), and Leroy Grumman, himself a former

First of the monoplane cats was the F4F Wildcat, still retaining the patent landing gear. This one, a General Motors-built example, an FM-2, is about to take off at Oshkosh.

Navy pilot, insisted that in any aeroplane bearing his name, the cockpit should be the last area to fail. Trainee Hellcat pilots must have felt reassured to watch a training movie (since repeated often on television) which showed a returning Hellcat miss the arrester wires and go spinning into the carrier's island losing both wings, the engine and finally the entire tail section, leaving the pilot sitting uninjured in the undamaged cockpit section.

It was the Hellcat which finally established American air dominance in the Pacific, first on 17/18 February 1944 when F6F-3s attacked Truk and destroyed 127 Japanese aircraft in the air and another 86 on the ground, and most decisively on 19 June 1944 when more than 400 Japanese bombers heading for the US fleet were intercepted by Hellcats. All but 18 of the enemy aircraft were shot down in an engagement which came to be known as the Marianas Turkey Shoot, so easily did the Japanese fall to the Grummans.

US Navy Hellcats ended the war with a total destruction tally of 4947 aircraft out of a grand total of 6477 enemy aircraft destroyed by all US Navy types, and with a kill to loss ratio of 19.1 to 1 it was the most successful carrier-based fighter of the war. Three of the four top-ranking US Navy fighter aces were Hellcat fliers. Commander David McCampbell from USS Essex destroyed 34 Japanese aircraft, nine of them in one engagement; Lieutenant Cecil Harris who flew with VF-18 and VF-27 Squadrons scored 24, including three four-victory missions; and Lieutenant Eugene Valencia of VF-9 Squadron (known as the 'Mowing Machine' for its destructiveness) shot down 23 Japanese, including three out of six Zeros which attacked his Hellcat when he became separated from other aircraft in his group.

The Hellcat was the very personification of the term Air Superiority Fighter, but even so it lacked the speed and agility of the best Japanese types at low altitude. To fill this gap Grumman began work in 1943 on a lightweight fighter, aiming for the smallest airframe which could accommodate a 2400hp Pratt & Witney engine. It was to be the last of the great piston-engined 'cats', but although Grumman had a prototype XF8F-1 Bearcat flying by 21 August 1944 – 10 months after receiving an order from the US Navy – the aircraft was just too late to see wartime action, a pity for it might have been one of the greatest combat aircraft, with a rate of climb in excess of 500 feet per minute and such manoeuvrability that Grumman's engineering department devised a novel 'break-away' wingtip designed to fail midway between tip and wing-fold line if the aircraft exceeded 9g. The remaining wing area would withstand higher stress and was adequate to keep the Bearcat aloft.

Initial orders for 400 F8F-1s placed during the war were cut back after VJ Day and production finally totalled only 1254, of which 353 were taller-finned F8F-2s. Gulf Oil Company's aviation manager Major Al Williams owned a specially built civilian Bearcat called *Gulfhawk IV* which he used for aerobatic demonstrations in peacetime, and the US Navy's Blue Angels demonstration team also used Bearcats before re-equipping with Panther jets. Rebuilt surplus Bearcats were supplied to the French Armée de L'Air and to the Air Forces of Thailand and Vietnam.

Bearcats are the most numerous of surviving Grumman 'Cats' and have figured prominently in unlimited-class air racing in the United States. Darryl Greenamyer, a Lockheed test pilot, modified an F8F-2 with clipped wings, cut-down canopy and an airframe which was virtually a bare shell, stripped of every unnecessary piece of equipment. Powered by a specially prepared 2500hp DC-6 airliner engine driving an absurdly oversize propeller from a Douglas Skyraider, Greenamyer's Bearcat streaked low across the Mojave Desert in California in August 1969 to beat the world speed record for piston-engined aircraft set 30 years before by Germany's Flugkapitan Fritz Wendel's Messerschmitt Bf 109R. Greenamyer's average speed was 483.04mph, and his record remains unbroken. This Bearcat, *Conquest One*, is now an important part of the American National Air & Space Museum collection in Washington DC.

Here the final member of the family, an F8F-2 Bearcat, with conventional undercarriage, lines up at Oshkosh to follow the FM-2 into the air.

HAWKER HURRICANE

Rarely has an aircraft instilled such confidence among its creators that they have prepared to produce it by the thousand without a single order on the books, but so it was with Hawker's Hurricane fighter. Early in 1934 Sydney Camm, who headed the company's design team, was working on a monoplane successor to his Hawker Fury biplane to be powered by a steam-cooled 660hp Rolls-Royce Goshawk engine when he heard news of a new Rolls-Royce PV-12 engine which promised 60 percent more power with a single-stage supercharger.

The proposed 280mph 'Fury Monoplane' was quickly redesigned around the new powerplant and submitted to the Air Ministry as a potential replacement for the Royal Air Force's ageing fleet of front-line biplanes. The Ministry's specification had called for armament of eight licence-built American Colt-Browning .303 calibre machine guns, but Camm's Interceptor Monoplane had only four guns, so in August 1934 a new Ministry specification was drawn up around his design and detailed submissions were made which promised a top speed of 330mph at 15,000 feet — far in excess of then-current RAF types.

Powered by the newly named Merlin engine, the prototype F.36/34 fighter first flew on 6 November 1935 with Hawker's chief test pilot P W S 'George' Bulman at the controls. Though the hump-backed thick-winged monoplane differed from Camm's original concept in having retractable landing gear, it retained the simple fabric-covered steel-tube structure and fixed-pitch wooden propeller of his biplane designs. Camm had his doubts about the aircraft, confiding later that he had feared it would be a failure; with more time he believed he could have designed a thinner wing which would have made the Hurricane the greatest fighter of all time.

Hawker's chairman, Thomas (later Sir Thomas) Sopwith, was so impressed, however, that he ordered raw materials and bought-in components for an unprecedented 100 airframes

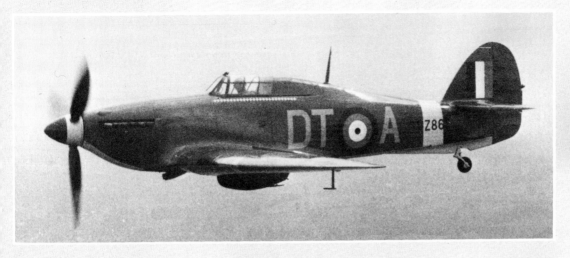

One of the two flying Hurricanes of the Battle of Britain Memorial Flight, a Mk IIc and the last of about 14,000 Hurricanes built, carrying the markings of Wing Commander Stanford-Tuck of 257 (Burma) Squadron.

in March 1936 before even the RAF had conducted trials or placed an order. Mindful of developments in Germany, Sopwith had gambled, and three months later his gamble paid off handsomely when the Air Ministry ordered 600 aircraft—fewer than expected but still the largest-ever peacetime order for a British aeroplane. The name, Hurricane, was officially approved for the fighter, which had reached a speed of 316mph at 16,000 feet during trials at the British Aircraft & Armament Experimental Establishment at Martlesham Heath in September 1936.

Despite setbacks with delivery of the Merlin

engines which delayed the RAF Fighter Command's plan to have 500 Hurricanes in service by March 1939, the first Hurricanes (by then fitted with the eight Brownings) were delivered to 111 Squadron at RAF Northolt near London less than two months after the first flight of a production aircraft, and within eight weeks, all 16 of the squadron's aircraft were operational, reflecting both the faith of the manufacturers and service chiefs and the growing tension in Europe. On 10 February 1938 Squadron Leader John 'Downwind' Gillan, Commanding Officer 111 Squadron, did much to boost public confi-

Strathallan Collection's Hawker Hurricane is a Mark IIb 12-gun example built in Canada and restored in the UK to represent the 605 Squadron aircraft flown by Squadron Leader Archie McKellar DSO DFC, one of the men who contributed to the Hurricane's fame.

dence in the RAF's new fighter when he flew his Hurricane from Edinburgh to Northolt at an average groundspeed of an astonishing 408mph. Euphoric publicity made no mention of the 60mph tailwind.

When the Munich crisis blew up in September 1938 three RAF squadrons were equipped with Hurricanes and production at Hawker's Brooklands factory was running at eight per week. Two months later an order for 100 more was placed and Hawker negotiated co-production agreements with the Gloster Aircraft Company and with the Canadian Car & Foundry Corporation in Canada to meet the demand. By the time of the Battle of Britain 2309 Hurricanes had been delivered to 32 RAF squadrons.

It is one of those unfair ironies of fate that while the Spitfire remains synonymous with the Battle of Britain, Hurricanes shot down more enemy aircraft in action than all the other fighters combined, with the highest-scoring Hurricane ace, Polish Sergeant Josef František, downing 17 German aeroplanes in one month of that tense hot summer. While Spitfires took on the fighters, to the Hurricanes fell the less glamorous but more important task of attacking the Luftwaffe bomber formations as they swept in from the Continent. The head-on attacks employed against bombers by some Hurricane squadrons proved especially devastating.

Though 30mph slower than the early marks of Spitfire, the Hurricane was more flexible in its deployment, having an outdated structure which was more familiar to any RAF airframe fitter than the delicate all-metal monocoque of the Spitfire. It was easy to work on (Lord Beaverbrook's Civil Repair Organisation, which patched up combat-damaged aircraft and returned them to the front, once replaced both wings and all eight guns on a Hurricane in 115 minutes), its wide-track landing gear was more suited to rough grass airfields and bomb-damaged runways than the narrow-track legs of the Spitfire, and its less sensitive handling on approach was especially welcome to tired fighter pilots at the end of a long day of scrambles.

The 'Hurribox' was always popular with pilots. Its hump-backed cockpit gave excellent forward visibility, and thanks to that wide undercarriage it was much less prone to swing on take-off than a Spitfire (the RAF's Battle of Britain Flight's new pilots fly solo on a Hurricane before they are allowed to fly Spitfires), while control harmonisation was better than that of the Spitfire, which had heavy ailerons and a feather-light elevater response.

As a gun platform the Hurricane was superbly stable (though the recoil of the four 20mm cannon fitted to late marks would slow the aircraft by 30mph), and the close-mounted Brownings gave good concentration of fire so that a two-second burst from the 1000-rounds-a-minute guns was usually enough to bring down a bomber. The Merlin's float carburetter was at a disadvantage in dogfights with fuel-injection Messerschmitt Bf 109s, which could be pushed over into steep dives, whereas a Hurricane (or Spitfire) pilot had to half-roll and pull through or negative *g* would starve the Merlin of fuel and cause it to misfire; either way the 109 would get away.

The Hurricane never underwent the extended improvement and development of the Spitfire. Total production of all marks came to 14,231. Fewer than two dozen still exist, and just three are airworthy, including the 14,231st, 'The Last of the Many', which was delivered to the RAF in September 1944, was returned to the manufacturers as a company 'hack' and is now back in military hands again with the Battle of Britain Memorial Flight at RAF Coningsby.

The Battle of Britain Flight has two Hurricanes, restored in the colours of aircraft flown by Wing Commander Bob Stanford-Tuck, one-time Commanding Officer of 257 (Burma) Squadron, and of Group Captain Douglas Bader who commanded 242 Squadron during the Battle of Britain.

An airworthy Hurricane is thus a rare and priceless warbird. Just one is in private hands. A 12-gun Canadian-built example, it belongs to wealthy farmer and avid aeroplane collector Sir William Roberts at Strathallan, Perthshire. His Hurricane was discovered on an Edmonton, Alberta, scrapheap by a Royal Canadian Air Force pilot who bought it as a job-lot, rebuilt it without official help, and taught himself to fly it.

In 1968 the Hurricane came to England for the movie, *The Battle of Britain*, where Vivian Bellamy, a film pilot, discovered that this Hurricane flew not at all like those he remembered from his wartime days. It had a cut-down propeller from a Catalina amphibian, swung uncharacteristically on take-off, and trailed lengths of rope from its ailerons, ostensibly to balance the surfaces. Apparently the Canadian restorer had replaced the rotted original ailerons with new surfaces built by eye, for he had no drawings, and later when the machine was test-flown at Strathallan by Hawker's Duncan Simpson he discovered that the ailerons were so overbalanced that they would go full

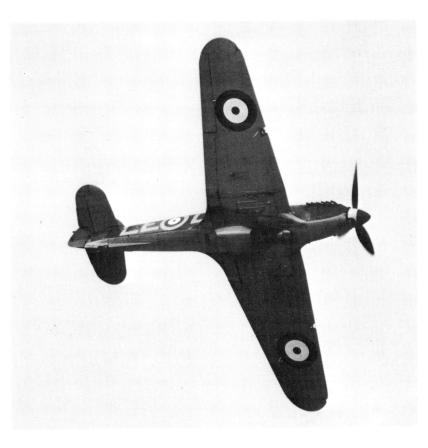

Battle of Britain Flight's other Hurricane, also a IIc, in the markings of Group Captain Douglas Bader when he commanded 242 Squadron during the famous battle.

deflection the moment he let go of the control column. They have now been replaced with ailerons as designed by Sydney Camm.

The Strathallan Hurricane flies in the colours of Scottish ace, Flight Lieutenant Archie McKellar, who shot down 21 German aircraft in his brief three-month career before he was killed in action in November 1940. Sir William Roberts finds his precious Hurricane more appealing than a Spitfire (he has one of those, too). 'A very British aircraft,' he says.

HEINKEL HE III

Few farmers in the flatlands of Cambridgeshire could have failed to recognise the shape of the two bombers which swept low over their fields that spring afternoon, nor the black crosses beneath their wings as they headed for the wartime Royal Air Force station at Duxford. The Spitfire and Hurricane which rose to meet them must have looked familiar too and given casual observers an uneasy feeling of *déjà vu*, for the year was not 1940, but 1968 and the British pilots were not shooting but waving at the incoming raiders.

Those 'in the know' would have realised that the Heinkels and their Messerschmitt escorts were arriving in Cambridgeshire for the making of the movie *The Battle of Britain*, but even so there can be little doubt that more than a few

shuddered to see again the sinister silhouette which became all too familiar to the people of Britain in the war years.

The Heinkel He 111 was developed as a twin-engined outgrowth of the record-breaking He 70 high-speed mailplane and retained its streamlined smooth-skinned lines. The prototype first flew in secret on 24 February 1935, followed two weeks later by a supposed 'civil' transport version for Deutsche Lufthansa. The German airline's fleet of He 111s subsequently made reconnaissance flights over Russia, France and Great Britain in prewar years while operating passenger and mail services (though in fairness the British Secret Service and French Deuxième Bureau were doing the same thing over Germany with ostensibly 'civil' aeroplanes).

For its day the Heinkel was a very advanced aeroplane and the first modern bomber to enter service with the Luftwaffe. Like the Junkers Ju 52/3m, the He 111 was tested operationally during the Spanish Civil War, when 30 880hp Daimler-Benz-engined He 111B-1s were sent to form the bomber group of the Condor Legion and proved most successful, not least because the 200mph-plus bomber was able to evade intercepting fighters by speed alone, leading Göring and his Luftwaffe colleagues to conclude erroneously that huge fleets of fast medium bombers would be invincible.

Thus it was that waves of Heinkel He 111s spearheaded the Blitz which was supposed to soften up Britain for the Nazi invasion. But the lightly armed bombers (Heinkels initially had just three 7.9mm defensive machine guns, one in the nose and one each at dorsal and ventral positions) proved easy prey for Royal Air Force fighters during the Battle of Britain, and proved beyond doubt to the Luftwaffe high command that speed alone was not sufficient protection in daylight raids.

Despite its failure as a strategic weapon during the Battle of Britain, the Heinkel He 111 was built in ever-increasing numbers. Twice production was halted then resumed again when planned replacements proved unsuccessful, and to the end of the war the old 'Spaten (Spade)' soldiered on, re-engined and re-armed, although the swift heels which it showed to Republican fighters in Spain grew ever slower as the weight of defensive armament, bombload and crew went up.

Heinkels remained in active military service even into the late 1960s, not with the Luftwaffe but in Spain, where the government aircraft factory CASA had obtained licence-production rights to the He 111H-16 in 1941 and added

Above: CASA-built Heinkel He 111 with US registration, demonstrating at Blackbushe after restoration and before delivery to its new American owner.

Right: And another He 111 that has already made the crossing and flies regularly in representative German markings with the CAF (Confederate Air Force) in Texas.

another 200 aircraft to the German total of more than 7000 before the last aircraft came off the line in 1956. The Spaniards replaced the Junkers Jumo engines, which had been manufactured from poor-quality short-life materials, with Rolls-Royce Merlins, a strange irony for it was the Merlin-engined Spitfires and Hurricanes of the RAF which first clipped the fast-flying bomber's wings.

Despite their British engines, which lack the distinctive throbbing note of the unsynchronised Daimler Benz and Junkers powerplants, the Spanish Heinkels are very Germanic aeroplanes, characterised by the streamlined 'greenhouse' nose which afforded no protection for the crew and hampered rather than aided visibility. In bright sunlight one gets the impression of being in a fair-ground mirror maze with infuriating reflections leering back from the many-faceted nose, while in bad weather the visibility becomes so bad that on some variants the pilot's seat and controls could be raised to permit him to poke his head through an openable panel in the roof for landing. The glasshouse must however have been an excellent platform for bomb aimers, and has since provided a much-overused frame for movie shots of London burning during the Blitz.

That aside, the Heinkel was a popular aeroplane with Luftwaffe crews for its docility, honesty and ease of handling, which reduced crew workloads at times when the last thing they needed was a recalcitrant aeroplane.

JUNKERS JU 52/3M

Motorists journeying between London and the Hampshire town of Basingstoke in 1980 might be forgiven for thinking that they had entered a time warp, or that the Nazi invasion which never came in 1940 has happened at last, for alongside the road at Blackbushe Airport stand four Junkers Ju 52/3m trimotor troop transports bearing the splinter camouflage, crosses and swastikas of the Luftwaffe.

The 'Tante Jus' (Auntie Junkers, as they were popularly known) brought no paratroopers though; indeed, despite their disguises, they are not German aircraft at all, but licence-built copies manufactured by the Spanish company Construcciones Aeronauticas SA (CASA) for the Spanish Air Force, and they belong to British warbirds collector Doug Arnold, who also has a hangar piled nearly to the roof with the world's biggest collection of Ju 52 spares.

The Junkers, along with the Ford Trimotor and Douglas DC-3, ranks as one of the most famous of all transport aircraft, and one of the longest serving. The first prototype Ju 52 was the culmination of 11 years of continuous development which started in 1919 with the Junkers F13, a four-passenger aircraft which played a major role in establishing air routes throughout the world. The first Ju 52 flew on 13 October 1930 and initial production aircraft were single-engined. It was not until 1932 that Junkers designer Ernst Zindel capitalised on the aeroplane's success by installing three licence-built Pratt & Whitney Hornet radial engines in the airframe and unwittingly produced an enduring classic, characterised by the thick cantilever wings and load-bearing corrugated skin which was a Junkers hallmark and earned the aeroplane the nickname 'Iron Annie'.

The first production Ju 52/3ms were sold to a Bolivian airline which used them as military transports during a war with Paraguay in 1932/33; immediately the Junkers' ruggedness was put to a stern test when Bolivian pilots flew them into rocky jungle airstrips whose 'runways' consisted of thousands of cowhides strewn on the ground by local cattlemen.

The German national airline Deutsche Lufthansa equipped itself with Ju 52/3ms, eventually owning no fewer than 230 of them, many of them named after the great fighter aces of the

The corrugated skin, full-span ailerons and massive span of nearly 100ft are well shown in this picture of one of the Blackbushe Junkers Ju 52/3ms.

Great War — *Richthofen, Udet, Boelke*. One, named *XI Olympiade* and bearing the five linked-rings symbol alongside the Nazi swastika, was used to transport the Olympic Flame from Greece to Berlin for the 1936 Olympic Games. Another plushly equipped aircraft was reserved for the personal use of the Führer himself. Ju 52s eventually formed 85 percent of Lufthansa's fleet and served with airlines of nearly 30 countries in Europe, Asia, Africa and South America.

While 'Iron Annies' were winging sturdily and safely around the world a bomber variant was developed for the clandestine Luftwaffe, armed with a pair of MG15 machine guns, one of which was mounted in a retractable 'dustbin' turret beneath the rear fuselage. Twenty Ju 52/3 bombers were sent to Spain in 1936 with the Condor Legion, and it was during the Spanish Civil War that the aeroplane's toughness really proved its worth. The Ju 52s were used at the outset to transport Moorish troops to Spain from Morocco, and later bombed Republican towns in the Mediterranean. Nicknamed 'Pava (Turkey)' by the Spanish, Nationalist Ju 52s flew 5400 missions and dropped 6000 tons of bombs for the loss of only five aircraft in aerial combat, one of which succumbed only after attack by two dozen Republican Polikarpov I-15 biplane fighters.

But it was during World War II that 'Tante Jus' performed most valiantly. Hordes of them swarmed across Denmark and Norway during Operation Weserübung carrying nearly 30,000 men, 2376 tons of supplies and a quarter of a million gallons of fuel. In May 1940 475 Ju 52s took part in the invasion of Belgium, France and Holland, where many of the selected landing zones were blocked by trenches and hastily dug pits.

One Ju 52 pilot landed on a long narrow tree-lined road and taxied fully two miles, smashing the trees flat with his corrugated wings so that the remaining aircraft could land safely. Others took off again on burst tyres, running on the wheel rims alone, and at least one flew away with a nine-foot section of outboard wing missing. A total of 157 'Tante Jus' was lost to anti-aircraft fire during the five-day campaign in the Netherlands. Ju 52s continued to spearhead German campaigns throughout the war, in the Balkans, on the Russian Front and in the Western Dessert.

And in peace the old girl was far from finished. In France Ateliers Aeronautiques de Colombes continued production that had begun during the German occupation and supplied Ju 52s to the French Air Force, Navy and national carrier Air France, while CASA in Spain added a further

Smokey burn-off of inhibiting oil as the port unit of the newly installed Wasp engines of one of the 'Iron Annies' is started.

170 'Iron Annies' to the German total of 4845 aircraft. Captured Ju 52s formed part of British European Airways' immediate postwar fleet, entering service on the Croydon-Liverpool-Belfast route in November 1946. Until recently 'Iron Annies' were active in commercial use in New Guinea and South America, and three are still serving with the Swiss Air Force, perhaps because no modern aircraft can offer the rugged load-carrying capability of the old trimotor and perhaps out of pure sentimentalism.

The secret of the Ju 52's success and longevity is that it was immensely strong, almost certain to survive the roughest controlled forced landing, and that it was an agreeable aeroplane to fly thanks to that thick Teutonic wing with its full-span ailerons and slotted flaps – Junkers's 'Double Wing' concept – which bestowed it with remarkable short take-off and landing charac-

Proprietorial satisfaction is evinced by Doug Arnold as all three engines warm up.

teristics and slow-flight capability. The gap between wing and control surfaces could cause problems in cold weather, however. Ice tended to accumulate quickly between the surfaces and swiftly led to loss of control unless the pilot kept up a constant wing-waggle to prevent the ailerons from freezing solid.

I have never actually flown in an 'Iron Annie', but I have taxied around an airfield in one. I have great respect for the Wehrmacht troops who travelled to war in them, for that flying nissen hut is quite the noisiest machine ever, its corrugated flanks amplifying every discordant note of the three unsynchronised Pratt & Whitney Wasps with which Doug Arnold's Spanish-built examples have been re-engined. But shake and shudder though she might, one could at least be sure that 'Tante Jus' would never fall apart; she was a tough old bird.

SPITFIRE

He created a legend, but like many a masterpiece-maker Reginald J Mitchell never knew it. Mitchell won fame though no fortune with his seaplane designs for the Schneider Trophy Races in the 1920s. His Supermarine S6B won the Trophy outright with a third consecutive British victory in 1931 at 340.08mph, and set a world speed record of 407.5mph when there was no longer any competition to beat.

In the 1930s Mitchell knew as much as any man about the special problems of high-speed flight. Even before that conclusive 1931 victory he had in mind a fighter design to make use of the Rolls-Royce Goshawk engine, but Mitchell was ill-pleased with his Supermarine 224. The ministerial specification to which it was designed had been too constricting, denying him the free-handed scope he needed, and the crank-winged open-cockpit fighter with its fixed undercarriage and 600hp steam-cooled engine served only to inspire further development.

In private Mitchell began to redesign the aeroplane the way *he* thought it ought to be, unfettered by the demands of 'desk-top fliers'.

The pure poetry of line of Mitchell's Spitfire is well depicted in this picture of one of the RAF Battle of Britain Flight's restored machines.

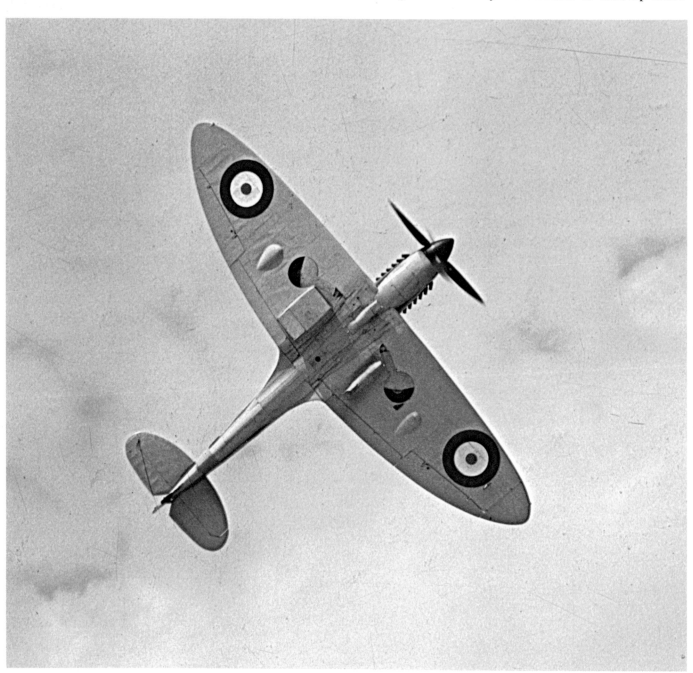

He had drafted two Goshawk-powered variants with enclosed cockpits and retractable landing gears when Rolls-Royce announced the new 1000hp PV12 engine and the Air Ministry issued yet another specification, calling for an eight-gun fighter capable of flying at 275mph at 33,000 feet. Mitchell rearranged his design around the compact new engine to produce a sleek impressively elegant aircraft with a thin elliptical wing. He called it Supermarine Type 300. In January 1935 an eager Air Ministry awarded a prototype contract and – like that for Sydney Camm's Hurricane – drew up a specification around the Supermarine design.

The prototype flew on 5 March 1936 from Eastleigh Airport, near Southampton. Test pilot 'Mutt' Summers was immediately impressed with the aircraft's handling and within weeks the Spitfire-to-be had flown at 350mph. Two months later an initial order for 310 Spitfire Mark Is was placed for the RAF, followed by another 200 aircraft in 1937. Mitchell was never to see a production Spitfire fly. Even as the light-blue prototype lifted off the grass on that day in the spring of 1936 he was dying of stomach cancer, and although he bravely worked on, bearing the brunt of production-standard design work, Mitchell finally succumbed on 11 June 1937.

Unlike the Hurricane's conventional steel-tube and fabric structure, the Spitfire's all-metal monocoque fuselage and stressed-skin wings with complex curvatures and subtleties did not lend itself readily to mass-production. It has been estimated that one Spitfire took 330,000 man-hours to build — the equivalent of three normal working lifetimes. The small Supermarine factory at Woolston, on Southampton Water, could not cope with demand. Nine or 10 subcontractors were hired to manufacture Spitfire parts, but even so they were hard pressed, and late in 1937 a 'shadow' factory was established at Castle Bromwich, near Birmingham. The new factory immediately received an order for another 1000 aircraft before the building itself had been erected.

Early Spitfire Is were similar to the prototype, but as a result of service experience a number of improvements were made. Flush exhausts were replaced with triple ejector units, the tailskid by a castoring tailwheel, and a 1030hp Merlin II engine was installed driving a three-blade two-speed propeller in place of the original two-blade fixed-pitch unit. Early in 1939 a domed cockpit canopy was introduced and an external bullet-proof windshield was added at the insistence of RAF Fighter Command chief Hugh 'Stuffy'

Dowding, who observed wryly: 'If Chicago gangsters can ride behind bullet-proof glass I see no reason why my pilots should not do so too.'

Spitfires first saw action on 16 October 1939 when aircraft from 601 and 603 Squadrons intercepted Luftwaffe Heinkel He 111s over the Firth of Forth, bringing down the first enemy aircraft over British territory. Two weeks later the same units shot down another Heinkel which crashed on the Lammermuir Hills near Dalkeith and was the first Luftwaffe aircraft actually to crash on British soil.

When the Battle of Britain started in July 1940 RAF Fighter Command had 19 squadrons of Spitfires, eight of them based with 11 Group in the south of England. Production was running at five aircraft a day — less than half the rate achieved for the easier-to-build Hurricane — but as the battle progressed the repair programmes instituted by Lord Beaverbrook were turning out replacements at the rate of 188 per week.

It was a shortage of trained pilots, not aeroplanes, which posed the greater problem. The 'young chicks' who comprised Winston Churchill's beloved 'Few' were fledglings indeed, mostly in their teens or early twenties and desperately undertrained. If they came to a front-line Spitfire squadron with more than a dozen hours solo on the aircraft they were well off. Many had little experience of anything but low-power fixed-undercarriage trainers. They were poor marksmen. Survival was a matter of learning fast or dying, and although the Spitfire enjoys a legendary reputation from the Battle of Britain, it was a small group of experienced aces, such

Imposing business-end shot of a privately owned Mk 1a, one of the oldest airworthy Spitfires, which is based at Booker in Buckinghamshire.

as 65 Squadron's Paddy Finucane and 74 Squadron's famed South African fighter tactician 'Sailor' Malan, who did most of the scoring.

The Spitfires' task was primarily to fly top cover against the Luftwaffe's Messerschmitt escort fighters while the slower Hurricanes attacked the invading bombers. The Spitfire 1A was just marginally faster than a Bf 109E, and with greater wing area could turn more steeply and tightly if its pilot dared pull enough g. Most, used to slow unresponsive trainers, would back off under the unfamiliar and uncomfortable g loads, giving the advantage to the more-experienced Luftwaffe fliers. At altitudes above 20,000 feet the German fighter was superior, and could escape from a Spitfire by pushing over into a high-speed dive; the Bf 109E had direct fuel

injection, whereas the Merlins in Spitfires and Hurricanes were fed by float carburetters. For all that, Spitfires achieved remarkable victories against formidable odds. German ace Adolf Galland, when asked by Reichsmarschall Hermann Göring what he most needed to beat the RAF, allegedly replied 'a squadron of Spitfires'.

One area in which those first (and all) Spitfires excelled was in handling. They were fast, accelerated rapidly and had beautifully harmonised controls that were light except at high speeds when the ailerons (especially) became heavy. But for sheer joy of flight, for exuberant 'oneness' betwixt man and machine, few aircraft have ever rivalled Mitchell's masterpiece, though some of those early pilots found the change from tractable trainers to slippery Supermarines just too

Contrast in Spitfire wing forms — Mitchell's pleasing ellipse of the Mark IX, privately owned and based at Booker; and the most widely used clipped C wing of the Shuttleworth Trust's Mark V.

much and there were many accidents.

To discourage carelessness fines were imposed on inexperienced pilots who damaged their Spitfires — five shillings for taxiing with flaps down, overheating the Merlin or buckling a propeller; £5 for landing with the wheels up, which everyone did sooner or later. The money went to the ground crews who had to repair the aircraft. They grew rich and pilots grew careful, especially in ground handling the Spitfire on its narrow-track undercarriage, and during take-off when over enthusiastic application of power would persuade the aircraft to swap ends abruptly.

Production of the Spitfires ran through two dozen major marks for the RAF and totalled more than 20,000. A Spitfire is, rightly or wrongly, the most coveted warbird of all, sought after by any collector worthy of the name and with a bank balance to suit. I would not like to guess how much an airworthy example might cost, for buyers are notoriously reticent about such matters, but I have seen one advertised for a quarter of a million dollars and was told that it was cheap at the price. And yet a Spitfire is not that rare. There are at least 50 preserved examples in Britain alone, of which eight are flying at the time of writing and others are under active restoration.

The RAF still owns the most airworthy Spitfires: a Mark IIa, a Mark V and two PR XIXs with the Battle of Britain Memorial Flight. However, collector Doug Arnold, who has a museum of flyable warbirds at Blackbushe Airport, might one day be the Spitfire 'king'. He has an air-

One of the four Spitfires regularly flown by the Battle of Britain Memorial Flight, a PR XIX.

worthy Mark IX and no fewer than four others recovered derelict from India being rebuilt on a veritable production line in a Blackbushe hangar. The oldest airworthy Spitfire is the Honourable Patrick Lindsay's Mark 1A, which shares a hangar at Wycombe Air Park with Cathay Pacific airline chief Adrian Swire's Mark IX. Swire's Spitfire is the only one fully cleared for aerobatics (one must be careful with old air-frames), and thus the only one capable of performing publicly as a Spitfire should.

In the hands of Ray Hanna, who flies for Cathay Pacific and also gets his hands on the boss's most cherished aeroplane, the Spitfire's performance is joyous, lyrical and moving. He starts with a shallow dive along the crowd line to little more than shoulder height, pulling up into a half-loop, the Merlin popping as the car-buretter gives up under negative g at the top, rolls out, loops, flies wing-over to show that lovely elliptical shape, rolling out of a three-quarter loop and turning tightly among the trees before another low-level turn and a climbing victory roll away into the distance – a continuous curving display which emulates the free-flowing unbroken lines of the aeroplane and leaves the crowd begging for more.

What was the magic of Mitchell's design that it should still enrapture small children, children whose parents scarcely remember that summer of 1940? Essentially it was the right aircraft at the right time, a distinctive shape coupled to an evocative defiant name which boosted morale and symbolised the courage of a nation.

P-51 MUSTANG

Even with earplugs the noise is painful; the heat wafting back through the firewall from the Merlin catches my breath and the g force drags at the skin on my face as we swoop down onto the target. There he is dead ahead, black crosses showing clearly on the tops of his wings. We close up. He tries to break right, but we turn inside him and in the instant that our windscreen frames his stubby silhouette I press an imaginary gun button and smoke billows from beneath his radial engine. Another kill. But this was no Fw 190, just a USAF-surplus North American T-28 trainer not too convincingly disguised with Luft-waffe markings, 'A sheep in Wulf's clothing' playing at war games. A real Fw 190 would not have been such easy meat even for the Mustang.

Paradoxically, the Mustang, archetypal American fighter of World War II, owed its existence to the British. In the spring of 1940 the British Government's New York-based Purchas-ing Commission needed as many American fighters as they could get for the Royal Air Force. They needed them very badly, but the Curtiss factory simply could not cope with orders for its P-40 Tomahawk which the RAF favoured. Thus the Purchasing Commission set off for California to meet James H 'Dutch' Kindelberger, president of North American Aviation to ask if the com-pany would care to manufacture Tomahawks under licence. Kindelberger declined but re-quested that his company be allowed to design an entirely new fighter. The British agreed to return in four months to examine the new aircraft.

And so Kindelberger, chief engineer John Atwood and designers, Ray Rice and Ed Schmeud, designed and built the prototype NA-73X fighter in 177 days. It first flew on 26 October 1940 powered by an Allison V1710 liquid-cooled inline engine, which proved troublesome at high altitude in production air-craft and hampered an aeroplane which was otherwise vastly superior to contemporary fighters on both sides of the Atlantic. In the autumn of 1942 Major Thomas Hitchcock, US Air Attaché in London, suggested that the Mustang's high-altitude performance would benefit from the substitution of a British Rolls-Royce engine. Trials with an experimental installation produced a top speed of 433mph and prompted an order from the United States Army Air Force for P-51B Mustangs.

In USAAF service the Merlin-powered Mus-tang quickly excelled as an escort fighter, accom-panying B-17s and B-24s on round-trip missions ranging 1000 miles or more, but the early P-51B and C models were hampered by lack of firepower from their four Browning .50s and poor combat visibility, particularly to the rear. Two P-51Bs were experimentally fitted with streamlined teardrop canopies similar to those fitted to the Hawker Typhoon and this version, designated P-51D, was to become the most prolific of all Mustangs. In addition to the bubble canopy the P-51D had strengthened wings to carry six guns and un uprated 1695hp Packard-built Merlin engine. Devastatingly effective in ground attack, the P-15D could also out-perform any German fighters at altitude and had phenomenal range – 2000 or more miles when equipped with external droptanks – enabling the Mustangs to go all the way to Berlin and back from their English bases.

When the first P-51Ds arrived at Eighth Air

Force units in Britain in May 1944 they were enthusiastically received by pilots weaned on the heavier and clumsy P-47 Thunderbolt. The Mustang was easy to fly, but it was not docile. As in any aeroplane, over-confidence could kill. So manoeuvrable was the P-51 that the main limiting factor was the pilots tolerance of *g* forces. Late in the war USAAF Mustang pilots were kitted out with the first anti-*g* suits which squeezed their bodies during high-*g* manoeuvres to prevent blood surging and blackouts. Thus equipped P-51D pilots were able to make such tight turns and steep pull-ups that their aeroplanes sometimes came back with markedly more wing dihedral than they started out with and fewer rivets.

Although in the fading months of the war in the European theatre the Mustang escort fighters frequently met little opposition on their far-ranging 'little friend' missions (the bombers were 'big friends'), and much of that from inexperienced, reckless and demoralised Luftwaffe pilots, the P-51D acquitted itself well in combat. Lieutenant Chuck Yeager, who later became the first man to exceed Mach 1 in level flight aboard the Bell X-1 rocket aircraft, destroyed five Messerschmitt 109s on one October day in 1944, while Captain Bill Wisner of the 352nd Fighter Group downed six Fw 190s on 21 November 1944. Major George Preddy of the 532nd Fighter Group was the highest scoring Mustang ace of

the war with 24 kills, six of them on one day, but he died on Christmas Day 1944 after his P-51 was hit by anti-aircraft fire.

Mustangs even scored against the rocket and jet fighters which the Luftwaffe sent up as a last desperate attempt to stop the massed bomber formations of the USAAF. On 16 August 1944 Lieutenant-Colonel John Murphy of the 359th destroyed an Me 163 Komet over Leipzig; on 7 October a P-51D pilot destroyed two unidentified Luftwaffe fighters over northern Germany before even realising that they were Me 262 jets, and a month later Eighth Air Force Mustangs shot down Walter Novotny, a 250-kill ace, and three of his colleagues from an Me 262 unit. Between 1944 and 1945 Mustangs accounted for nearly half of all the enemy aircraft destroyed by USAAF pilots in Europe – 9081 in 13 months, of which 4950 were shot down in aerial combat.

In all 15,586 Mustangs were built, 7956 of them P-51Ds. After the war's end they were supplied to foreign air forces, some of whom still operate the type. Others were disposed of for as little as $3500 each — one-fifteenth of their original cost. Many were snapped up for air racing and figured prominently in the postwar National Air Races at Cleveland, Ohio. Paul Mantz, the great movie flier who died tragically and wastefully during the making of *The Flight of the Phoenix*, became the only man ever to win the Bendix Trophy race three times, with a P-51C.

Like many of the airworthy Mustangs, this privately owned P-51D based with the Confederate Air Force taking off at Oshkosh in 1978 has been modified to take a passenger seat behind the pilot.

Another privately owned P-51D, in wartime markings and rather optimistically named *Passion Wagon*, airborne for its role in the mock battle played out at Oshkosh airshow.

He had installed in his Mustang a 'wet' wing (in which the fuel is contained within the sealed wing structure rather than in conventional tanks) and filled and polished the exterior to a mirror-bright finish. Charles Blair, a Pan American Airways captain, bought the aircraft from Mantz and flew it nonstop from New York to London on 31 January 1951 in seven hours 48 minutes, later returning westbound to make the first ever solo crossing of the North Pole.

Later a passenger on one of his scheduled Stratocruiser flights across the Atlantic stopped him in the aisle. 'Captain,' he said, 'did you hear about that guy who flew the Atlantic solo in an old World War II fighter? He must be mad.' 'Must be,' Blair assured him.

Mustangs are still raced, but many more are owned by the unlikeliest people, – doctors, lawyers, accountants, businessmen, many of them ex-USAAF fliers, who swap business suits at weekends for an old pair of combat fatigues and re-acquaint themselves with the big-macho fighter. Years ago, when Mustangs were still cheap, so many people bought them and killed themselves trying to fly them that the US Federal Aviation Agency became very worried about the whole business of private ownership of ex-

warplanes. In a two-year period inexperienced pilots with little or no flight time in high-performance aircraft wiped out one-third of the entire US P-51 population. One pilot who carried five people in his, climbed so high that they all passed out from oxygen starvation and tore the P-51 apart as it nosed over into a near-supersonic dive.

Today, with the price-tag on the humblest airworthy P-51 running at around $100,000, such recklessness is rare, and happily many of the surviving Mustangs have been modified as two-seaters (the passenger sits behind the pilot in the position formerly occupied by a fuel tank, armour-plate and radio equipment) so that the P-51 is one of the few single-seat fighters which the casual rider can sample first hand, even if somewhat cramped. Noise and heat assail you and the tall, inexperienced and unready get their heads cracked against the canopy during high-speed manoeuvres (many USAAF pilots had trouble sitting high enough to see out of the big bubble hood and were categorised as one-, two- or three-cushion fliers according to how much bolstering their stature demanded), but it is a breathtaking experience in all senses, raw power and performance, the mark of a thoroughbred.

CORSAIR

American Marines clawing their way across the bloody islands of the Pacific in 1945 knew it as the 'Okinawa Sweetheart'. Japanese at the receiving end of its tremendous firepower called it 'Whistling Death'. And rookie US Navy and Fleet Air Arm pilots dubbed it the 'Bent-Wing Bastard from Connecticut'.

Chance Vought's Corsair fighter was the result of a US Navy specification issued in February 1938 for a single-seat shipboard fighter plane. Designers Rex Beisel and Igor Sikorsky selected the most powerful engine then available – an 18-cylinder 1850hp Pratt & Whitney Double Wasp XR2800 – and immediately encountered their first problem. To make use of all that power the experimental XR2800 needed a massive 13-foot diameter Hamilton Standard propeller. Big propellers need long landing gears for ground clearance, and long spindly undercarriages are ill-suited for the jarring unflared arrivals of heavy aeroplanes on aircraft carrier decks.

The solution provided the Corsair's most popular and derogatory nickname, the 'Bent-Wing Bastard from Connecticut'. The inverted gull wing, however, permitted the use of short sturdy undercarriage legs, with side benefits of improved over-wing visibility and a low-drag wing/fuselage junction. The prototype XF4U-1 flew on 29 May 1940. On 11 October it became the first American fighter to exceed 400mph in level flight. The following month the US Navy revised its requirements in the light of combat reports filtering through from the war in Europe, and the original armament specification of two fuselage-mounted .30s and two wing-mounted .50s was increased first to four .50s in the wings and later to six wing guns. To accommodate the increased ammunition load fuel tanks were relocated from the centre section to the fuselage and the cockpit position was shifted farther aft,

destroying the fine visibility provided by the 'bent-wing' feature and leading to piloting problems which delayed the fighter's service entry.

By September 1942 the first US Marine Corps Corsair squadron, VMF-124, was equipped with the aircraft, carrier trials had begun, and so had the problems. Cockpit visibility through the framed canopy was poor for carrier operations and the stiff undercarriage legs provoked bouncing on touch-down causing the Corsair to go springing across the deck over every arrester wire and into the crash barrier. The US Navy thus rejected the F4U-1 for seagoing operations initially and it fell to the shore-based Marine Corps units to blood the aircraft in combat, beginning in February 1943 from Henderson Field on Guadalcanal. But even on land the Corsair was not easy to handle. The throttle needed the most delicate touch, and many trainee pilots coming to Corsair units from SNJ trainers quickly gained respect for the powerful torque effect of its 2000hp R-2800 engine and huge paddle-bladed propeller. Suddenly opening up to full throttle during a simulated carrier deck 'wave-off' could roll the F4U-1 inverted and drop it straight into the ground unless the pilot countered the torque with a bootful of rudder.

The Corsair would ground-loop on landing too, a fact to which the author can offer personal testimony. While shooting pictures for this book at the edge of a runway during an airshow in the United States I unwisely turned my back on the action while reloading a camera. A piercing *screech* of protesting rubber and metal grabbed

A good illustration of the 'bent-wing' method adopted by Chance Vought to keep the Corsair fighter's propeller from fouling the ground or deck.

An F4U-ID Corsair fighter/
bomber, one of the many
privately owned machines
based at Rebel Field,
Harlingen, Texas, which
regularly take part in
Confederate Air Force
airshows.

my attention very quickly and I turned in time to see a big navy-blue Corsair come pirouetting off the tarmac and onto the grass towards me in a cloud of dust. Luckily the pilot managed to get it stopped after a couple of turns with no damage done.

Directional stability during the landing roll-out was improved on the F4U-1A model introduced from the 689th airframe, as was cockpit visibility. A small spoiler on the starboard wing's leading edge aided the pilot while rolling on the ground, and a raised clear-view canopy replaced the old 'greenhouse'. Still the US Navy refused to approve the Corsair for carrier operations, even though the British Fleet Air Arm had happily been flying their Lend-Lease Corsairs off and onto small escort carriers, and it was not until the spring of 1944 that US Navy ships finally began to receive fully operational deck-landing-approved F4Us after a protracted modification and test programme to take the bounce out of the aircraft's undercarriage.

The Corsair was the most important naval attack aircraft of World War II and enjoyed the longest continuous production run of any contemporary American fighter. Production of the F4U-1 was completed in February 1945, but developed versions remained on the assembly lines of Vought and Goodyear (subcontractors) until December 1952 when the last of 12,582 aircraft was completed – an 11-year production record equalled only by McDonnell Douglas's F-4 Phantom jet fighter.

In combat the Corsair proved mightily effective; against the Japanese only 189 Corsairs were lost for 2140 enemy aircraft destroyed. VF-17 squadron of the US Navy, which was the first unit to operate Corsairs and the service's highest-scoring outfit of the war, destroyed 154 enemy aircraft in 79 days and produced a dozen aces with five or more kills apiece. Pilots from the squadron providing aerial cover for the aircraft carriers USS *Essex* and USS *Bunker Hill* during the first strike against Rabaul in 1943 destroyed 18 Japanese torpedo bombers and – a nice touch of irony this – successfully landed the entire squadron on one of the carriers when lack of fuel prevented them from reaching their land bases.

Top scorer among VF-17 'Skull and Cross-bones' Squadron's many aces was Lieutenant Ira Kepford, with 19 kills. All but one of the 2140 Japanese aircraft destroyed were shot down. The exception was literally sawn apart by Lieutenant R Klingman of the US Marine Corps whose guns jammed during an attack on a Japanese 'Nick' bomber over Okinawa. Flying Leathernecks did not like to be beaten, so Klingman formed up in tight line astern and let his big Hamilton Standard propeller chew off the bomber's tail surfaces.

A few years ago I spotted a crowd around a preserved Corsair at an American warbirds gathering. In the cockpit sat a man with the lined leathery face of one who has lived long and hard; squinting thoughtfully at the sun while camera shutters snapped around him and youngsters (and more than a few oldsters) proffered autograph books and pens. It was Colonel Gregory Boyington, the legendary 'Pappy' Boyington who commanded the best-known Marine Corps Corsair squadron – VMF-214, the 'Black Sheep' Squadron.

Boyington served with Claire Chennault's Flying Tigers in China. He was a flamboyant, hard-drinking, hard-living, hard-fighting flier whose band of irreverent outlaw pilots gave almost as much trouble to the Marine Corps' top brass as they did to the Japanese, but they shot down more enemy aircraft than any other USMC outfit and 'Pappy' himself ended up as the top-scoring Corsair ace with 28 kills. 'She was a real sweetheart,' he says wistfully, patting the flanks of the Corsair painted in VMF-214's old colours for a television series based on his book *Baa Baa Black Sheep*.

The Corsair left its mark on postwar history, too. In 1949 former navy pilot Cook Cleland won the Thompson Trophy Race at Cleveland, Ohio, in a much-modified Goodyear-built F2G Corsair. Cleland bought the F2G for $1250, stripped it of every piece of unnecessary equipment, cropped four feet off each wingtip to improve an already high roll rate, and used hydrogen peroxide injection to boost its 3000hp Wasp Major engine to 4500hp. Cleland won the 15-lap race at a record average speed of 397.071mph; two other F2Gs placed second and third. It must have been a wild ride; to get the modified F2G's centre of gravity where it should have been Cleland had to carry 100 gallons of water ballast in the rear of the aircraft.

Cleland once taught a lady pilot to fly his Corsair by crouching behind the single seat and flying the aeroplane with a broom handle fastened to the control column. His Thompson Trophy-winning Corsair still exists, the property of an eccentric collector in Ohio who keeps it and many other historic aircraft in his backyard, steadfastly refusing all offers from museums and restorers while the aircraft grow rusty.

How best to sum up the Corsair? In the words of a Marine on Iwo Jima: 'We owed our lives to those funny looking bent-wing birds.'

WARBIRDS: A REVIEW

Left: The Grumman TBF Avenger torpedo bomber, which started its active service in the Midway battles in June 1942, made a major contribution to the outcome of the war. It was easy to manage aboard carriers and could carry 2000lb of bombs or torpedoes at up to 270mph. It was used also by the British Fleet Air Arm, with whom it was named Tarpon up to 1944 when the American name was standardised. This one is flown with the CAF (Confederate Air Force) in Texas.

Below: The Ryan Company's name is known chiefly as the builder of Lindbergh's 1927 solo Atlantic aircraft *Spirit of St Louis* but it also produced a noteworthy series of primary trainers, PT-16, -20, -21, -22 and -25, used widely by the USN and USAAF and other countries. Pictured is a privately owned PT-22 at a 1978 Oshkosh meet.

The Messerschmitt Bf 109,
which first flew in 1935,
was the only German
World War II fighter built
in quantity and perhaps
not surprisingly, therefore,
it was built in greater
numbers than any other
single type of aircraft.
The exact number built is
not known but the total
appears to have been well
in excess of 30,000. The
one pictured is a Spanish-
built Rolls-Royce Merlin-
powered version maintained
by the Confederate Air
Force in representative
Luftwaffe markings.

Above: The most noted and successful of Japanese World War II aircraft was the Mitsubishi AGM Zero-sen, known as the Navy O to the RAF in Malaya and the Arakan and codenamed 'Zeke' after the US entry into the war. The Zero dominated the eastern skies until it was eventually outmatched by the Grumman F6F Hellcat in 1943. This picture shows an NA T-6 converted to represent a Zero for the film *Tora! Tora! Tora!*

Left: The Fairey Firefly carrier fighter/recce aircraft was introduced in 1943 and more than 1700 were built between then and the end of the 1940s. The Mark 5 Firefly here pictured taking off is the Fleet Air Arm Historic Flight's example finished in the markings of 814 Squadron, with which it started its service life during the Korean War.

Another restored airworthy example of the Lockheed twin-boom P-38 Lightning about to take off during a CAF (Confederate Air Force) display.

The Curtiss P-40 Warhawk was the first mass-produced US single-seat fighter and with the Bell P-39 formed the basic USAAF fighter strength during the early war years; it was also supplied in bulk to other Allied air forces including the Russian. The one pictured flies from the CAF field at Harlingen and demonstrates the suitability of the P-40's frontal shape for fearsome decoration.

A most prolific maid-of-all-work warbird was the North American AT-6 Texan, an armed flying classroom used in the training of many thousands of service aircrew in about 40 countries. Records vary of the number built but it was probably as many as 15,000, of which around 5000 were RAF Harvards. This picture shows an AT-6D Texan of the Strathallan Collection.

The all-round most-potent US fighter of World War II was the twin-engined Lockheed P-38 long-range fighter, which was responsible for destroying more Japanese aircraft in the Pacific area than any other type. It was also used in light bomber and recce roles. The one pictured is demonstrating its remarkably quiet performance at its CAF home ground in Texas.

All antique aeroplane owners are collectors in their way, even the man with just a single machine, but for the purpose of this chapter I have selected only those collections which are readily available to the public view (like art collectors who keep their treasures in bank vaults, some antique enthusiasts keep their aeroplanes locked away from prying eyes). The list is by no means exhaustive. At any airfield you may come across an antique or two, but most of the bigger collections are mentioned here.

Maintaining collections of airworthy antique aeroplanes is a relatively modern concept, and largely financed by private individuals or by charitable trusts. National bodies have been singularly lapse in the preservation of aircraft other than as static museum exhibits, perhaps because of a notion that rare aeroplanes, particularly sole surviving examples, are just too vulnerable to risk. Certainly some unique aeroplanes have been lost in flying accidents, including the one and only Bristol Bulldog which rolled itself into a sad ball of crumpled wood, metal and fabric very publicly at a Farnborough Air Show, but my feeling is that aeroplanes belong in their proper element, the air, where successive generations can see them as they should be seen — flying.

Previous page: A formation seen less frequently, although the individual aircraft — Sea Furry and Firefly from the RN Fleet Air Arm Historic Flight and Hurricane and Spitfire from the BBMF — are individually much in evidence during the season.

Impressive line-up of colourful Mustangs, mostly privately owned, assembled for the 1978 Oshkosh fly-in.

CONFEDERATE AIR FORCE

Everyone in the Rio Grande Valley, Texas, knows Colonel Jethro E Culpepper. He's a fine figure of a man, tall, tanned, with a shock of white hair and a little goatee beard that makes him look a lot like that other Southern gentleman, Colonel Saunders of Kentucky Fried Chicken fame. Curiously, however, although everyone along the Gulf coast knows Culpepper, no one has ever actually *seen* him. The reason is that Colonel Jethro E Culpepper, Commander of the Confederate Air Force Ghost Squadron, does not exist; he is himself a ghost, a myth, but his air force is very real.

The Confederate Air Force dates back to the early 1950s when founder Lloyd Nolen began pining for his Army Air Corps days and the adrenalin-pumping thrill of flying high-performance fighters. Nolen and some good buddies got together and bought themselves a surplus P-51 Mustang and flew it on weekends. Someone jokingly suggested that they should call themselves the Confederate Air Force, and since everyone in the real Air Force always seemed to rank at least as high as colonel, they began commissioning themselves 'colonels' and even designed CAF uniforms — in Rebel Grey!

By 1963 they had one example of each of the major American fighter types of World War II which were helping to pay for their (expensive) upkeep by performing at airshows. By 1968 the arrival of bombers in the collection forced a move from the original field at Mercedes, to a former Army Air Corps base at Harlingen, now renamed Rebel Field.

The CAF is an extraordinary organisation in the grand Texan manner. There are about 3500 commissioned 'colonels' worldwide, 17 regional 'wings' and a full-time staff of 20 to cater for the day-to-day needs of more than 60 flyable aircraft, the world's largest collection of airworthy warbirds. The CAF is a non-profit organisation which pays its way through membership fees and donations from the colonels, many of whom have put up five-figure, and in some cases six-figure, sums to sponsor individual aircraft purchases or cover restoration and maintenance costs of such aircraft when located.

Paying out big money does not buy the right to fly any of the aircraft. CAF pilots are closely vetted, their progress is recorded on proficiency sheets just like a real air force, and they are categorised as: Pilots, who may only make cross-country flights; Senior Pilots, who are permitted to make straight-and-level demonstration passes; and Command Pilots, with full low-level formation and aerobatics privileges. There are no exceptions, and to encourage responsible flying,

One of the regular performers at CAF airshows is this Bell P-39 Airacobra; with engine behind the pilot, the propeller is driven by a shaft passing through the cockpit.

CAF colonels are expected to pay for repairs should they be unfortunate enough to damage an aeroplane.

Non-flying colonels help out in a wide variety of support roles. Volunteers are always needed for maintenance, electrical work, painting, logistics, historical research, even cooking and baking for the men. Those who perform beyond the call of duty may receive the ultimate accolade, a mention in dispatches from 'Good Ol' Colonel Culpepper' himself. Those who disgrace themselves, perhaps by ground-looping an aeroplane on landing, receive the most dishonourable Order of the Brass Jackass from the Colonel, who hands them out readily to anyone who steals his reserved parking spot alongside his private mint patch from which he is said to make the most exquisite mint juleps.

The quasi-military stance of the CAF (which ranks high among the world's air forces for numbers of aircraft owned) is essentially a 'fun thing', frequently misunderstood by anti-war groups. The colonels' real purpose is simply to preserve an important part of their heritage in a readily identifiable and exciting way; 'living monuments' they call their aeroplanes. From the early days, when warbird-owning pilots gained bad reputations for their devil-may-care flying, the CAF has grown into a responsible and highly respected organisation through whose efforts and ingenuity all-but-forgotten aircraft have been recovered from remote spots around the world, rebuilt and flown again. Where else in the world can you see airworthy B-17s, B-24s and B-29s flying in formation, or an F-82 Twin Mustang, a Douglas Dauntless or Curtiss Helldiver, or four Messerschmitt 109s (albeit Merlin-engined Spanish-built ones) or Airacobras and Kingcobras, Wildcats and Hellcats, Havocs and Marauders?

How does the CAF find its treasures? Mostly by word-of-mouth, rumour and whispers, from a worldwide network of spies on the lookout for undiscovered warbirds. Six P-47 Thunderbolts were discovered in Peru and bought by Ed Jurist, a vintage car dealer from New York who now does an equally busy trade in warbirds and has worked closely with the CAF. His latest and greatest coup has been the purchase of no fewer than 24 Hawker Fury fighters from Iraq; Jurist also negotiated the deal which brought an airworthy de Havilland Mosquito across the Atlantic to Harlingen, although the aircraft has since been traded back to a British collector.

The highlight of the Confederate Air Force is the annual airshow, held in October and (justifiably) billed as the world's most exciting aerial spectacle. 'Colonels' from all over the Americas bring their warbirds to Harlingen for this get-together, and the CAF mess cooks brew up cauldrons of lethally hot chilli and beans.

The show starts each afternoon at three o'clock prompt. A voice drawls out over the flightline loudspeaker 'Gen'lemen, y'all kin start yo' engines!' The colonels use the Texas skies as an aerial stage not just for fly-bys but for carefully choreographed re-enactments of the most famous aerial battles – the Spanish Civil War, the bombing of Poland, Battle of Britain, Chennault's Flying Tigers in China, the Eighth Air Force daylight raids on Germany, the disastrous low-level raids on the Ploesti oil refineries, Doolittle's Tokyo Raid, the air-sea Battle of Midway and so on, recalling the sorties of yesteryear.

The noise subsides. Over the public address comes soft Hawaiian guitar music. 'It is Sunday 7 December 1941, a warm peaceful morning here at Honolulu . . .' The rest of the message goes unheard as across the field stream formations of fighters and torpedo bombers bearing the red 'meatball' markings of the Japanese Imperial Navy. A fireball erupts on the airfield, followed by another and another.

The Japanese have attacked Pearl Harbor. Rebel Field, Harlingen, has been transformed into Hickam Field, Hawaii, the CAF colonels scramble to a Grumman Wildcat and a pair of P-40 Warhawks while the Zeros, Vals and Kates, most convincingly converted from T-6 and BT-13 trainers, strafe the runway and colonel Bill McCoy, the CAF explosives expert, fires off

The CAF's Consolidated B-24 Liberator *Diamond Lil* is a reminder that the type was far more versatile and built in greater numbers (about 18,000) than its more-publicised running mate, the B-17.

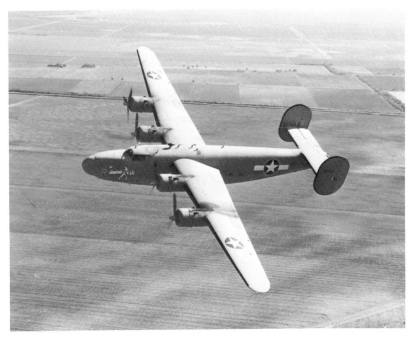

Left: At the 1975 CAF airshow – a gaggle of bombers comprised of Invader, Liberator, Superfortress and Fortress.

Bottom left: American World War II fighters, left from nearest camera: midship-engined Airacobra, Mustang and Corsair, at the 1975 CAF airshow.

Below: A Curtiss P-40 Warhawk entertains the 1978 CAF airshow crowds, its boudoir-pink paint-job belying the fearsome jaws contrived around the engine air intake.

A World War II oddity is commemorated by the CAF in this P-82 Twin Mustang. It was created by joining two P-51s with common centre main and tail planes to provide a more-effective long-range escort fighter. About 250 were built, mostly after the war ended.

another charge of dynamite and aviation fuel while a B-17 lumbers in with smoke pouring from the number two engine and one undercarriage leg jammed up.

An amazing spectacle it is, the grand finale of the CAF show, sometimes alternated with a rerun of the bombing of Hiroshima using the collection's flagship B-29 *FiFi*. The Japanese Government was greatly distressed when Colo-nel Paul Tibbets, commander of *Enola Gay* during the actual atomic bombing, rode in *FiFi* during the re-enactment in 1976. The US State Department thought an apology might smooth things over, but the CAF colonels pointed out that they were not about to apologise to anyone; after all, they noted quite reasonably, there had been no howls of protest in America over the Pearl Harbor re-enactment.

AIRWORTHY AIRCRAFT IN THE CONFEDERATE AIRFORCE COLLECTION

Lockheed P-38 Lightning
Bell P-39 Airacobra
Curtiss P-40 Warhawk
Republic P-47 Thunderbolt
North American P-51 Mustang
Bell P-63 Kingcobra
North American F-82 Twin Mustang
Goodyear FG-1D Corsair
General Motors FM-2 Wildcat
Grumman F6F Hellcat
Grumman F8F Bearcat
Grumman TBM Avenger
Curtiss SB2C Helldiver
Douglas SBD Dauntless

Supermarine Spitfire 9
Messerschmitt Bf 108
Messerschmitt Bf 109 (Spanish-built)
Aichi Val dive-bomber (replica)
Mitsubishi Zero (replica)
Nakajima Kate torpedo bomber (replica)
Boeing B-17 Flying Fortress
Douglas A-20 Havoc
Consolidated B-24 Liberator
North American B-25 Mitchell
Martin B-26 Marauder
Douglas A-26 Invader
Boeing B-29 Superfortress
Heinkel He 111 (Spanish-built)

Lockheed Lodestar
Consolidated PBY-5A Catalina
Douglas C-47 Skytrain
Beech C-45 Expediter
Beech AT-11 Kansan
North American T-6 Texan
Vultee BT-13
Boeing Stearman PT-17 Kaydet
Fairchild PT-19
Ryan PT-22
Stinson L-5 Sentinel
Fieseler Storch
Focke-Wulf Stieglitz
Junkers Ju 52/3m

OLD RHINEBECK

Cole Palen was a student at the Roosevelt Field School for Mechanics on Long Island just after World War II, and there mouldering in a hangar sat a shabby collection of Great War aeroplanes – an Aeromarine 35B, Avro 504K, Curtiss Jenny, Sopwith Snipe, SPAD S.XIII and a Standard J-1. In 1951 the school closed and Palen, dreaming that one day he might start a collection of old aeroplanes like the Shuttleworth Trust in England made a $500 offer for the machines, and became owner of all six.

The aeroplanes were stored in a Poughkeepsie, New York, barn and slowly restored. Then, in 1958, Palen bought up a derelict farm at Rhinebeck just off the Taconic State Parkway in upstate New York with the idea of starting a small airfield there and keeping the antique aeroplanes as a sideline. Over the next five years Palen was joined by other enthusiasts who shared his love for old flying machines and between them they created an airfield and hangars and acquired more aeroplanes – a 1909 Blériot XI, a 1912 Thomas Pusher, a Nieuport 28 used by Paramount Studios for movie work, a Fokker D-7 which Anthony Fokker apparently smuggled out of Germany after World War I and had been stored in a Massachusetts shop, and a Curtiss Jenny which arrived in two dozen pieces and did not fly again until 1969. Weekend airshows run by a band of faithful volunteers, who often outnumbered the paying patrons, helped defray some of the expenses.

Cole Palen's collection was one of the first private museums of airworthy antique aeroplanes in the world, and since then it has burgeoned into one of the best. The former farm has taken on the appearance and ambience of an early aerodrome, perfectly complemented by a fine and varied collection of aeroplanes and replicas from the 1900–1937 period and contemporary vintage vehicles, owned both by the Collection and by private owners caught up in the unique Old Rhinebeck atmosphere.

In particular Rhinebeck's collection of World War I aeroplanes has no rival save for the still-to-be-completed Leisure Sport flying circus in England. Apart from those founding machines acquired at bargain price from Roosevelt Field, most of which have finished their flying days and are displayed statically, Rhinebeck can boast a trio of flying Sopwiths – Pup, Camel and Dolphin – an Avro 504K replica, Albatros D Va replica,

Fokker Triplane replica, Royal Aircraft Factory FE.8 replica, and an original Thomas-Morse Scout which spent eight years at the USAF Museum at Wright-Patterson Air Force Base in Dayton, Ohio, before Palen acquired and restored it to flying condition.

The aerodrome is open every day of the week from mid-May to October, but to see the collection at its living best Sunday is the day to go, for then Cole Palen and his friends put on airshows which are pure theatre. Cast as the villainous Black Baron, Palen struts around the field eagerly pursuing the virtuous young maiden Trudy Truelove who in two decades has thus far escaped the ace's dishonourable intentions, while from the opposite camp comes the 'good guy', Sir Percy Goodfellow, played by Dick King, another Old Rhinebeck stalwart who built and owns the Sopwith Pup kept at the aerodrome.

The crowds who flock to Palen's 'Greatest Show Off Earth' love it and besiege their caricatured heroes for autographs.

The protagonists line up: Palen in the black and red Fokker Triplane, King in the Pup, Dashing Dick O'Day in the Camel, Stanley 'One-

A rare World War I bird seen to fly at Rhinebeck is this Airco (de Havilland) DH 2 replica, a Lewis gun-armed pusher type designed as a two-seater. The single-seat production DH 2 in the hands of a dexterous pilot could master the dreaded Fokker Eindecker.

Another of the Rhinebeck
originals was an Avro
504K. Here a 504K replica
is taking off to take part in
the comic melodrama that
forms a major Rhinebeck
attraction.

Inset: One of the Old
Rhinebeck Aerodromes
numerous flying World War
I aircraft and replicas, a
Sopwith Pup replica.

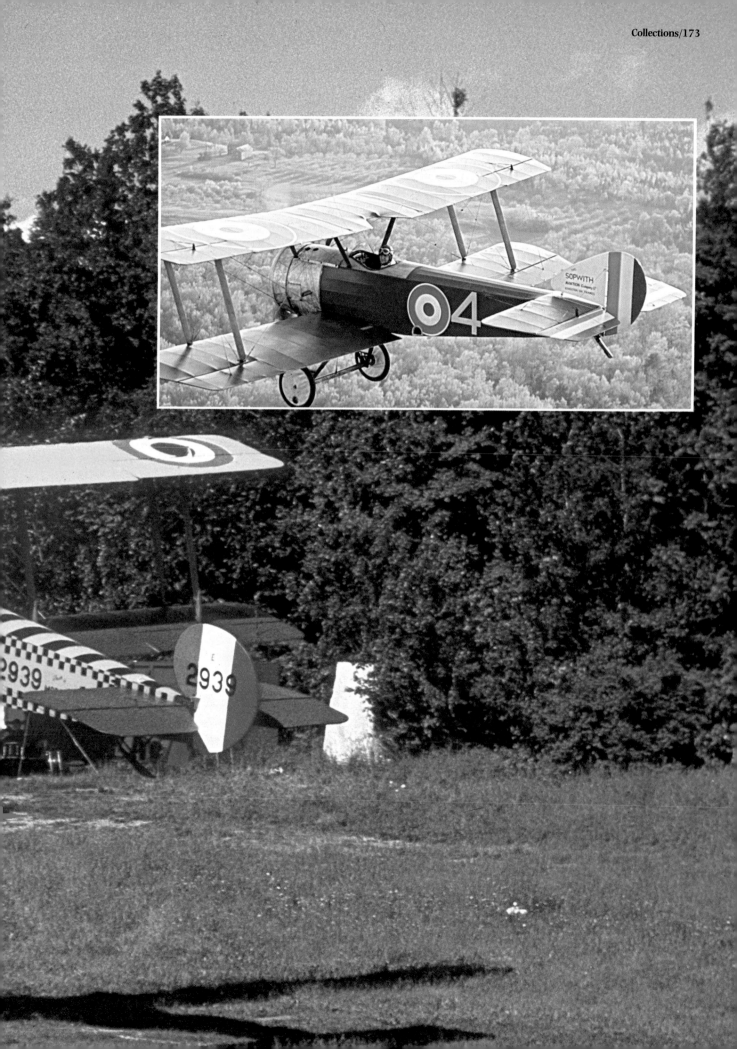

Another of the star performers in the Old Rhinebeck melodrama is this Fokker Dreidecker replica, in bold black and red paint for its pilot the Black Baron.

Shot' Segalla in the garish yellow and black chequered Avro 504K. The scenario is always the same. They wheel around firing mock machine guns while a helper on the ground adds some percussion and smoke for effect before the Black Baron, cad that he is, dispatches poor old Sir Percy with a well-aimed burst of Hispano (the crowd boos and hisses) then gets his 'come-uppance' at the hands of 'One Shot', whose mock Le Prieur rockets make short, if historically inaccurate, work of the Dreidecker (cheers from the masses).

AIRCRAFT OF THE OLD RHINEBECK COLLECTION

1918 Aeromarine 39B
1930 Aeromarine-Klemm
1937 Aeronca C-3*
Albatros DVa replica*
1917 Pigeon-Fraser Albree Scout
Avro 504K replica*
1931 Bird CK*
1909 Blériot XI
1910 Blériot XI*
1911 Blériot XI*
1911 Breguet
1910 Curtiss Pusher A
1911 Curtiss Pusher D*
1918 Curtiss Jenny*
1929 Curtiss Fledgling*
1931 Curtiss-Wright Junior*
1929 Davis D1-W*
1930 de Havilland Puss Moth
1913 Deperdussin Monocoque replica

1929 Dickson Glider*
1937 Fairchild 24
1942 Fleet Finch 16B*
RAF FE.8 replica*
1918 Fokker D.7*
Fokker DR1 replica*
1939 Funk B*
1930 Great Lakes Biplane*
1929 Monocoupe 113*
1932 Monocoupe 90*
1929 Morane-Saulnier MS.130*
1910 Hanriot Monoplane replica*
Nieuport 2N replica*
Nieuport 11 replica*
1917 Nieuport 28
Passat Ornithopter replica
1936 Piper J2 Cub*
1929 Pitcairn Mailwing*
1921 Raab-Katzenstein glider

Santos-Dumont Demoiselle replica
1910 Short S-29*
1918 Siemens-Schuckert D-III replica
1917 Sopwith Camel replica*
1916 Sopwith Pup replica*
1918 Sopwith Dolphin replica*
1918 Sopwith Snipe
1918 SPAD XIII
1929 Spartan C-3*
1918 Standard J-1
1917 Thomas-Morse S4B*
1911 Thomas Pusher I
1912 Thomas Pusher 2
1908 Voisin
1926 Waco 9
1928 Waco 10*

Asterisks indicate airworthiness

SALIS COLLECTION

If you visit French aerodromes you may notice people wearing little badges announcing that they are *Amis de Jean-Baptiste Salis*. The late Monsieur Salis was a man revered in France for the restoration of airworthy antique aircraft, not a particularly popular pastime among Gallic fliers because until recently French Aero Clubs have been encouraged by handsome government subsidies to throw away old aeroplanes and replace them with pristine new machines.

Jean-Bapiste Salis first flew an aeroplane in 1912 at the age of 12 and became a military instructor in the last year of the Great War before setting up an aircraft repair shop at Toussus-le-Noble, now the main general aviation airfield for the city of Paris. Just before World War II he bought a tract of land atop a plateau at la Ferté-Alais, about 40 kilometres south of the French capital, there to establish an airfield and a home for his collection of more than 30 aeroplanes, all of which were destroyed during the German occupation.

In the early 1950s Salis was working for the Musée de L'Air, France's national aeronautical collection, when he happened upon the remains of a Blériot XI Monoplane, which he rebuilt and twice flew across the English Channel in celebration of Louis Blériot's epic flight, once in 1954 and again on the 50th anniversary of the original

flight in 1959. This Blériot became the cornerstone of the Salis Collection, whose founder died in 1967. His son Jean took over from him, acquiring a second historic machine that same year, a World War I Caudron G-III observation and training biplane which was restored, after 10,000 hours of work, in time to take pride of place at the 1971 Paris Air Show, and it, too, subsequently crossed the Channel to England for the making of a television documentary on the history of flight.

The Salis Collection has expanded rapidly since then, supported, as such ventures invariably are, by a band of enthusiastic 'amis' whose only reward is to see old aeroplanes flying again. Unlike the other collections described here, the Salis Collection is not open to the public in the traditional sense, though visitors to La Ferté-Alais can usually get permission to view the aeroplanes, which are given a public airing once a year at a grand airshow held towards the end of May or early in June.

It is worth making the trip, because Jean Salis has gathered some fascinating antiques and replicas about him, and La Ferté-Alais airshows always have that homely casual air that permeates French aviation. The emphasis naturally is on French aeroplanes, with a particularly fine assortment of Morane-Saulnier Parasol types — three replica Morane Type As, and several big MS. 230s, 315s and 317s. There is also a fine replica of the 1912 Deperdussin Monocoque racer, which was the first aircraft to exceed 200 kilometres an hour and won the prestigious Schneider and Gordon Bennett races in 1913.

The Salis Collection's Bréguet XIV replica pictured at the annual airshow at La Ferté Alais.

Top: The Salis Collection's Latécoère 17 replica fashioned from a derelict Norduyn Norseman for a French television series.

Above: A British-owned Morane-Saulnier MS.230 parasol monoplane, about to be started in the only way possible with many antique aircraft.

For all its years the Deperdussin is a strikingly modern looking machine, designed by Louis Béchéreau who was also responsible for the formidable SPAD scouts (see Chapter 2).

Curiously 'Jeanot' Salis does not yet have an airworthy SPAD, the most famous of French warplanes of the era, but he does have replicas of the Nieuport 11 and 17 and Fokker Triplane, built in Germany by Arthur Williams who has a veritable World War I aircraft factory going at his Williams Flugzeuge works in Gunzburg. Also to be found at La Ferté-Alais are Tiger Moths masquerading as German Aviatiks, and most convincing they look.

Salis's latest and most ambitious replica building projects came about as the result of a French television series on European aviation history, for which the TV company needed aeroplanes to represent the types operated by Aéropostale, forerunner of Air France, which pioneered airmail services from France throughout Africa and South America and numbered among its brave pilots the great French aviation pioneer and writer Antoine de St Exupéry, Guillaumet who walked for five days and four nights through blinding snow after a crash in the Andes, and Jean Mermoz, who forged routes across the South Atlantic, flying, recorded his friend St Exupéry, through huge black waterspouts like the pillars of a temple.

Such deeds deserve remembrance, but where to get the aeroplanes? No single example of the Potez 25s, Breguet XIVs or Latécoère 17s and 28s used by the Aéropostale men existed. Salis came to the rescue. From the derelict remains of an old Norduyn Norseman transport left behind by the US Army in World War II he and his colleagues fashioned a very passable Laté 17 replica, characterised by its tubby fuselage, parasol wing and sharp-pointed triangular fin. Only the Pratt & Whitney radial engine gives the game away. The Breguet XIV was more difficult, and had to be built from scratch in less than five months. Powered by a 450hp Hispano-Suiza engine, it proved to be a fine flier and having completed its filming obligations with the Laté in the Alps and North Africa is now part of the La Ferté-Alais collection.

JEAN SALIS COLLECTION AIRCRAFT

Abraham Iris	Fokker DR1 Triplane replica	Nieuport 11 replica
Auster Autocrat	Govin Taupin	Nieuport 17 replica
Blériot XI	Latécoère 17 replica	Nord 1002
Breguet XIV replica	Leopoldoff Colibri	Nord 1101 Noralpha
Bücker Bü 131 Jungmann	Mauboussin M.120	Nord 3202
Bücker Bü 133 Jungmeister	Mauboussin M.127	North American AT-6
Caudron G-III	Mauboussin M.130	North American T-28
Caudron 69	Morane-Saulnier A replica	Piper L-4 Cub
Caudron Luciole	Morane-Saulnier MS.130	Salmson Cri-Cri
Caudron Phalene	Morane-Saulnier MS.138	SIPA 121
Caudron 800	Morane-Saulnier MS.181	Stampe SV-4
Curtiss Pusher replica	Morane-Saulnier MS.230	Stearman PT-17
Deperdussin Monocoque replica	Morane-Saulnier MS.315	Stinson SR-10C Reliant
Dewoitine D.26	Morane-Saulnier MS.317	Stinson 108 Voyager
Dewoitine D.520	Morane-Saulnier MS.341	Zlin 326
de Havilland Tiger Moth	Morane-Saulnier MS.500	
Fairchild Argus	Morane-Saulnier MS.733	

SHANNON AIR MUSEUM

Sidney L Shannon Sr was for 20 years vice-president of Eastern Airlines in the United States, having pioneered the development of the airline with World War I ace, Captain Eddie Ricken-backer. His son, Sidney Jr, himself a pilot and operator of Shannon Airport, near Fredericksburg, Virginia, wanted to create a memorial to his father, who died in 1970. He chose to build an aircraft museum to have as curator octogenarian Captain Henry T 'Dick' Merrill, former barnstormer, night mail pilot, and Eastern Airlines captain, who retired in 1961 with 44,111 hours and 29 minutes of flying time logged and goodness knows how many more than that unrecorded — more than five years spent off this earth.

The Shannon Air Museum was opened in June 1976 and is one of the finest of the world's collections of airworthy antiques which includes rare examples of significant aircraft types from American aviation history. Sidney Shannon's first antique was acquired in 1953 from a Dayton, Ohio, flower shop (antiquers know better than to discount *any* rumours of old aeroplanes stored away, however unlikely the location). It was a 1914 Standard E-1 biplane, one of only two still in existence from a production total of 150 built as World War I trainers. Though fully restored, the Standard is so far the only aircraft in the collection which does not fly. 'If time permits I'd like to rig the thing properly and fly it . . . perhaps next year,' says assistant curator Merton Meade.

The Shannon Museum has the only original, airworthy SPAD scout still flying, a 1917 SPAD

Top: Unique is this 1936 Vultee V-1 *Lady Peace II*, named for the V-1 in which Shannon curator Dick Merrill set a US-UK record in 1936.

Above: Popular lightplanes of the 1930s were Aeroncas ('Flying Bathtubs'). The Shannon Museum has a rare C-2 model. This example is a C-3 still flying in the United States.

S.VII built by the Mann-Egerton company in Norwich, England, restored but wholly original with a 150hp Hispano-Suiza engine. 'Not,' says Meade, 'a particularly nice flying airplane. She's very sensitive, not overly stable and ungodly hot in the cockpit.' Equally rare is a 1927 Pitcairn Mailwing, one of only two surviving – the other is statically exhibited at the National Air & Space Museum in Washington DC – restored in the colours of Eastern Air Transport, the company with which curator Dick Merill began his airline career and which later became Eastern Airlines.

In May 1978 this aircraft retraced an original mail route from Shannon Airport to Philadelphia, Washington, Richmond, South Boston, Greenville, Greer, Atlanta, Macon, Waycross, Jacksonville, Daytona, Melbourne, West Palm Beach and Miami. As if to remind pilot Meade of how it was to fly the mail in the old days the 220hp Wright Whirlwind engine put a valve through a piston on the return trip and he had to make a forced landing on a highway, with no further damage done.

From the same era comes a 1929 Curtiss Robin of the type flown across the Atlantic in 1927 by Doug Corrigan, known thereafter as 'Wrong Way' Corrigan because he claimed he was really heading westward to California and misread his compass; a 1927 Travel Air 2000 – the much-loved 'Elephant Ear' Travel Air favoured by Hollywood movie makers for its striking similarity to the Fokker D.7; and the only airworthy Bellanca Skyrocket, which joined the Museum in the summer of 1979.

The Skyrocket is painted to resemble the Bellanca WB-2 *Columbia* used by Clarence Chamberlin and Charles Levine to fly from New York to Berlin two weeks after Charles Lindbergh made the first solo Atlantic crossing. Levine, who was not a licensed pilot, subsequently managed to fly the Bellanca by himself from Germany to Croydon Airport, near London, where he was persuaded to continue his homeward journey by sea. The Skyrocket is an impressive aeroplane. It will carry six people, almost jumps off the ground in about 350 feet and does climb

like a rocket, according to Merton Meade.

Sidney Shannon Jr also has examples of four popular light aircraft from the 1930s. One is an Aeronca C-2N Deluxe Scout. (Deluxe was a relative term when applied to Aeroncas, which were well known popularly as 'Flying Bathtubs', for they were at best basic aeroplanes; designer Jean Roché is alleged to have left the company when the marketing people suggested putting doors on his aeroplanes.) It is a fine example of that minimum aeroplane which was built both in the United States and in Britain and known for the extraordinary *nok-a-nok-nok* sound made by its two-cylinder 36hp engine, whence the common corruption of its name into the 'Air-Knocker'.

There are two Cubs at Shannon Airport, a very rare 1932 Taylor E-2 Cub rescued from a garage store in 1977, and an immaculate Piper J-3 in factory finish – Cub Yellow with black trim, the only way to paint a J-3. Furthermore, there is a splendid 1937 Stinson SR-10G Reliant Gull Wing which I rate high among the world's most beautiful aeroplanes, this one has been restored in the blue and orange colours it wore as an American Airlines executive transport, during which time the company's president, C R Smith, force-landed it in a swamp, and is the most-often-flown aircraft in the Museum, still as comfortable, reliable and fast as it was 40 years ago.

But one aeroplane dominates the Shannon collection, figuratively and literally. It is a monster of a machine with a massive 1000hp Wright Cyclone engine and the name *Lady Peace II* beneath the side windows of its weird-looking forward-raked cockpit. One might be forgiven for not being able to put a name to it immediately because only 27 such Vultee V-1s were built and just one – this one – still exists.

The Vultee was built in 1936 to the order of the newspaper tycoon William Randolph Hearst. Painted gold, with a plush interior and a cruise speed exceeding 200mph, it was the 'executive jet' of its day. Just before World War II the Hearst Special was sold in South America, where for two decades it carried everything from bananas to baboons and eventually reappeared tattered and torn in California in the early 1960s, hotly pursued by unpaid bills. In 1963 it turned up on tow behind a car at a garage run by Harold W Johnston of Pueblo, Colorado, and was dumped there, Johnston eventually becoming its owner at a sheriff's sale. He restored it, flying the unique aeroplane again on 1 May 1971 bearing the name *Spirit of Pueblo*.

The Vultee V-1A is very special to the Shannon Museum, for on 2 September 1936 a Vultee V-1A named *Lady Peace*, her wings filled with 50,000 ping-pong balls for buoyancy, set a transatlantic speed record flying from New York to England in 18 hours 38 minutes. The pilot was Captain Dick Merill, his companion and sponsor of the flight Harry Richman, a popular entertainer made famous by his song 'Puttin' on the Ritz'. (Dick Merrill made another fast trans-atlantic flight the following year when he flew a Lockheed Electra to London and back to collect the first pictures of the Coronation of King George VI.)

Merton Meade says of *Lady Peace II*, 'She'll carry ten people and is a lovely ship to fly. She'll cruise at about 150mph at a rather conservative 45 percent power setting, but she'll still burn almost 40 gallons an hour. Not inexpensive....' Perhaps not, but something you just cannot put a price on.

SHANNON AIR MUSEUM AIRCRAFT

1914 Standard E-1
1916 SPAD S.VII
1927 Pitcairn PA-5 Mailwing
1927 Travel Air 2000
1929 Curtiss-Roberson Robin J-1D
de Havilland Gipsy Moth
1932 Aeronca C-2N Deluxe Scout
1932 Taylor Cub E-2
1936 Vultee V-1A Special
1937 Stinson SR-10G Reliant
Bellanca Skyrocket
1945 Piper J-3 Cub
Bücker Bü 133 Jungmeister

Among many rare birds recovered and restored by the Shannon Air Museum is the 1927 Pitcairn Malwing, here seen with the Museum's assistant curator Merton Meade.

SHUTTLEWORTH TRUST

The road signs off the A1 trunk route from London to the North of England say simply 'Old Warden', but they could equally well point to the Mecca for antique aeroplane enthusiasts, for at Old Warden Aerodrome lives the first and still best-known museum of airworthy vintage aeroplanes – the Shuttleworth Collection.

Founder Richard Ormonde Shuttleworth was born and bred at Old Warden Park and began collecting early vehicles in the 1920s. His first aeroplane – not then a collector's item – was a 1927 de Havilland 60X Hermes Moth, which remains in the Collection, along with the very first vintage aircraft acquired by Shuttleworth in 1935, a 1909 Blériot XI Monoplane and a 1910 Deperdussin. Richard Shuttleworth was emphatic that his should be a living, working museum, that each vehicle and every aircraft should be maintained in full functioning order. After his death in a flying accident with the Royal Air Force in 1940 his mother formed the Trust which administers the Collection as a memorial to him, with the aim of furthering aeronautical education and practice.

The aim has been well realised, because apart from an unparalleled collection of airworthy historic aircraft and working vintage vehicles, the Shuttleworth Trust's hangars are a Pandora's Box of rare aeronautica. There one may find, among other evocative memorabilia, parts from the last great British airships – the successful private-enterprise R-100 and the disastrous 'Socialist' airship R-101 – browse among remnants of another great folly, the behemoth Brabazon airliner, or marvel at the shimmering insect-like aeroplanes from the huff-and-puff world of man-powered flight.

On flying days, which take place on the last Sundays of the month and on most public holidays throughout the summer and autumn, there are other delights. Here on trestle tables

Above: One of the
Shuttleworth gems is the
only genuine airworthy
German World War I
aircraft in Britain, this
1917 LVG CVI.

Left: The very first of the
famous Shuttleworth
Collection at Old Warden,
the 1927 DH 60X Hermes
Moth and 1898 Panhard-
Levasseur, both of which
are still regularly active.

signing autographs on fragments of silver fabric. She is Jean Batten, the first woman to fly solo across the south Atlantic and from England to New Zealand. The fabric scraps come from the Percival Gull which carried her across oceans in 1935/36 and is now being restored to flying condition at Old Warden. A flying day at Shuttleworth has a magical carnival atmosphere that never fails to excite the most jaded aeronautical palate.

But the aeroplanes are deservedly the stars of the show, because the Shuttleworth Trust's Collection covers a broader spectrum of aviation history than any other in the world, ranging from the faltering steps of the Edwardian era to the confident dash of the postwar years, from Boxkite to Spitfire and beyond, carefully choreographed by the Collection's manager David Ogilvy and flown by a select band of talented volunteer pilots, many of whom travel across the country at their own expense for the privilege. Significantly not one pilot on the Shuttleworth's (very short) list of approved fliers has ever voluntarily resigned.

The very highest standards of airmanship are maintained at Old Warden, not just among the display pilots, but also among those many visitors who arrive by air. I have heard red-faced offending fliers who have transgressed in some way given severe reprimands over the public address and seen them shuffle away in agonised embarrassment, but they come back again and rarely make the same mistake twice.

Many of the Shuttleworth Collection's treasured antiques have been dealt with elsewhere in the text, but here also you will find other delights. The Collection has the only genuine airworthy World War I German aircraft in Britain, a 1917 LVG CVI reconnaissance aircraft which was captured during the Great War and subsequently stored by the Air Ministry until it was placed on

set out in front of the hangars is a 'flea market' of aviation mementos — pistons from a Merlin engine ('Make fine ash-trays,' the man says); small chunks of a genuine 1909 Blériot Monoplane's main spar; lozenge-camouflaged squares of fabric from a World War I German aeroplane; fragments of red-painted plywood from the de Havilland Comet which won the 1934 England–Australia Air Race.

An entire fabric fuselage side from an Avro 504K complete with RAF roundel is being auctioned, reserve price £50, while inside a hangar a man with a portable stereo system is playing recordings of aircraft sounds so realistic that the *grrrreeooowww* of a Spitfire brings people running outside, eyes strained upward.

In another corner a striking blonde lady who no one could believe is all of 70 years of age is

This Shuttleworth treasure, a DH 53 Humming Bird, has a double rarity value, as the sole survivor of only 13 of de Havilland's first lightplane and as the prototype DH 53 built for the 1923 *Daily Mail* trials at Lympne.

permanent loan to Old Warden in 1966. The restoration task was daunting. Many vital parts were missing, not least the entire cooling system for its six-cylinder 230hp Benz water-cooled engine, which had to be rebuilt from scratch with only a sketch from an old issue of *Flight* magazine as a guide. Enthusiasm overcomes such obstacles, and after five painstaking years the LVG flew again in 1972. It makes a fine sight with varnished plywood fuselage and five-colour dyed lozenge pattern fabric, the puffing exhaust stack from the Benz jutting up like a rhinoceros's horn.

From the same year comes the Collection's splendid SE.5A scout which was discovered hanging in the roof of the Armstrong-Whitworth company's hangar at Coventry Airport and restored by apprentices at the Royal Aircraft Establishment, Farnborough, where the SE.5 was originally designed. Another major rebuild took place in 1975/76, for restoration is a continuing, repetitive process, and many such aircraft have been rebuilt several times over as deterioration of wooden structures and fabric covering takes its toll.

The Collection has a particularly fine range of de Havilland lightplanes; plans are in hand to build a new hangar to house examples of all Sir Geoffrey de Havilland's magnificent Moth derivatives. Already on hand are: the 1923 de Havilland DH 53 Humming Bird, an aeroplane which the great pioneer Sir Alan Cobham once flew to Brussels and abandoned on the way back when he noticed freight trains overtaking him, so modest was its performance on a 34hp engine; a unique 1924 DH 51 biplane *Miss Kenya*; Richard Shuttleworth's original DH 60X Moth; and, of course, a Tiger Moth.

On flying days their numbers are boosted by the private collection of Tony Haig-Thomas, a self-confessed sufferer from 'Moth-mania' who owns Gipsy, Puss, Tiger, Fox, Leopard and Hornet Moths, and a Moth Minor, all of which he has been known to launch into the air at once, and whose pilots, mindful of the stylish dress of the service formation teams like the Red Arrows, are rumoured to be demanding Moth uniforms for future appearances! All these aircraft will be kept at Old Warden when the de Havilland hangar is built, along with a Dragonfly and the Trust's Comet racer which is undergoing an extensive rebuild to flying condition.

The Comet, victor in the 1934 MacRobertson air race from Mildenhall, Suffolk, to Melbourne, Australia, in the hands of Scott and Campbell-Black, is the Collection's most ambitious and time-consuming restoration yet, for it was little more than an empty shell when acquired from the de Havilland Company in 1965, having last flown in 1938. It is hoped that when completed the Comet will retrace its original route to Melbourne for the 50th anniversary of the England–Australia race in 1984.

Another long-term project has been the restoration of one of the great classics of the Golden Era, a Hawker Hind light bomber presented to the Shuttleworth Collection in 1970 by the Royal Afghan Air Force and carried by road vehicle overland to Old Warden. One of the joys of the Collection is that you can see the restoration process as it happens, for the workshop areas are generally open to public viewing.

Richard Shuttleworth could not have known just what he was starting back in the 1920s, but antique aeroplane enthusiasts the world over owe him a debt of gratitude. Old Warden is a fitting memorial.

SHUTTLEWORTH TRUST AIRCRAFT

All airworthy or under active restoration

Auster AOP 9
Avro 504K
Avro Tutor
BA Swallow
Blackburn Monoplane
Blériot XI
Bristol Boxkite
Bristol F2B

Cierva C30A
Comper Swift
DH 51
DH 53 Humming Bird
DH 60X Hermes Moth
DH 82A Tiger Moth
DH 88 Comet (being restored)
Deperdussin Monoplane
English Electric Wren
Gloster Gladiator
Granger Archaeopteryx

Hawker Tomtit
Hawker Hind (under restoration)
LVG CVI
Miles Magister
Parnall Elf II
Percival Gull Six (under restoration)
Percival Provost
Roe Triplane Mark IV
RAF SE.5A
Sopwith Pup
Supermarine Spitfire V

STRATHALLAN

Gleneagles in Scotland is famous for its hotel and golf course, and also for a growing collection of antique aircraft maintained at Strathallan, the local airfield. Sir William Roberts who owns the Strathallan Collection, which is probably the largest owned by one man anywhere in the world, came into the business almost by chance. Seeking to buy an ex-Canadian Hawker Hurricane IIc left behind after the making of the movie *The Battle of Britain*, he found himself not only with the Hurricane but also with two Spitfires as the result of an 'instant air force' package deal. What else to do but start a collection!

Sir William's plan was to create a flyable collection, concentrating where possible on aircraft types which had been used in Royal Air Force service. Apart from the now-restored Hurricane, which is the only privately owned example in the world currently airworthy, the Strathallan Collection has pulled off some notable coups in retrieving aircraft from abroad. An ex-Royal Canadian Air Force Lancaster X bomber was flown across the Atlantic to Strathallan from Canada, whence also came the remains of four other rare machines – a Westland

Top: Strathallan Collection's Percival Provost, last of the RAF's piston-engined basic trainers, on a circuit during one of the Strathallan flying days.

Above: This Strathallan General Aircraft Cygnet is the only known survivor of its type – the first British aircraft with tricycle landing gear.

Left: Two of Strathallan's examples of basic training aircraft – a 1947 Fokker S.II Instructor with side-by-side cabin flies over a 1937 open-cockpit tandem Miles Magister.

Airborne again in early 1980 after extensive restoration in the Strathallan engineering shop, this Westland Lysander short take-off and landing Army co-operation aircraft is a Mark III – the type that was used by the Special Air Service ferrying intelligence agents to and from fields behind enemy lines.

Lysander which has since been totally rebuilt and joined the flying collection early in 1980, a Fairey Swordfish, Fairey Battle and Bristol Bolingbroke, all of which are the subjects of difficult and protracted restorations.

Sir William also has one of the two privately owned de Havilland Mosquitos flying in Europe, a veteran of the films *Mosquito Squadron* and *633 Squadron*, and a non-flying Lockheed Hudson recovered from Australia. Unique, though less well known, are a pair of British lightplanes whose RAF links are tenuous at best – the Reid and Sigrist Desford twin-engined trainer (Desford was the home base of the company, though the aeroplane was also known as the Bobsleigh because of its Cyrano-de-Bergerac-like nose which housed the pilot in a prone position, and succeeded the even more peculiarly named Snargasher), and the General Aircraft Cygnet, which was one of few 1930s light aircraft to have tricycle undercarriages and saw brief military service as a trainer for pilots converting to tricycle-geared American types such as the Bell Airacobra and Douglas Boston.

No British collection is worthy of the name without a selection of Moths. Sir William has some rare specimens including a Moth Minor, a faultlessly restored Leopard Moth complete down to its braided strap-hangs for the passengers and linen antimacassars embroidered with the DH symbol, and a de Havilland Dragon recovered from Australia before the Australian authorities blocked further exports of historic aircraft (while still importing other people's). Several other Moths bound for Strathallan from the Antipodes were literally stopped at the docks, where they might still be.

Though hardly an antique in the sense of this book, the Strathallan Collection's most remarkable acquisition was a de Havilland Comet 2R airliner formerly used by the RAF. It is 'remarkable' because the jetliner was *flown* into Strathallan, whose grass strip is only just over 3000 feet long. There were some white knuckles in the air and on the ground that day. . . .

STRATHALLAN COLLECTION

Airworthy aircraft

Avro Lancaster X (under restoration)
BA Swallow
de Havilland Tiger Moth
de Havilland Dragon Rapide
de Havilland Moth Minor
de Havilland Mosquito
de Havilland Leopard Moth
Fokker S.II
General Aircraft Cygnet 2
Hawker Hurricane IIB
Miles Magister
Miles Monarch
North American T-6
Percival Prentice
Percival Provost
Reid & Sigrist Desford
Westland Lysander

This pathetic package, representing a fair proportion of a World War II Fairey Firefly carrier-borne fighter, was pictured on its way to the Strathallan engineering department and illustrates the condition from which many a restored flying gem has emerged.

OTHER NOTEWORTHY COLLECTIONS OF AIRWORTHY ANTIQUE AEROPLANES

Battle of Britain Memorial Flight, RAF Coningsby, Lincolnshire.
Avro Lancaster B1
Hawker Hurricane IIc (two)
Supermarine Spitfire Mk IIa
Supermarine Spitfire Mk Vb
Supermarine Spitfire PR Mk XIX (two)

Fleet Air Arm Historic Flight, RNAS Yeovilton, Somerset.
de Havilland Tiger Moth
Fairey Swordfish
Fairey Flycatcher replica
Fairey Firefly Mk 5
Hawker Sea Fury FB 11
Hawker Sea Fury TT 20

A familiar and emotive sight in the skies of Britain during the airshow season, the RAF Battle of Britain Memorial Flight's Lancaster and one each of its two Hurricanes and four Spitfires.

Duxford Aviation Society, Duxford Aerodrome, Cambridgeshire.
Note: the Imperial War Museum houses a large collection here, mostly static exhibits, but many privately owned aircraft belonging to members of the DAS are in airworthy condition and include
Beech D-17S Staggerwing
Boeing B-17G Flying Fortress
Cessna 195
Douglas A-26 Invader
Dewoitine D.26
de Havilland Tiger Moth
de Havilland Dragon Rapide
North American T-6
Supermarine Spitfire Mk V (Shuttleworth aircraft)
Yakovlev YAK-11

Leisure Sport Collection, White Waltham Aerodrome, Berkshire (all flyable replicas).
Albatros D Va
Airco DH.2
Fokker DR1 Triplane
Fokker D.7
Sopwith 1½-Strutter

Sopwith Camel
SPAD S. XIII
Supermarine S.5 Seaplane (at Thorpe Water Park)

Warbirds of Great Britain, Blackbushe Airport (private collection of Douglas Arnold)
Boeing N2S-5 Stearman
CASA 352L (Spanish-built Junkers Ju 52/3m)
de Havilland Mosquito
Hawker Sea Fury TT 20
North American T-6
North American TB-25N Mitchell
North American P-51D Mustang
Republic P-47D Thunderbolt
Sopwith Pup
Supermarine Spitfire Mk IX (and four others under restoration)
Westland Lysander

Wycombe Air Park, Booker, Marlow, Buckinghamshire. (Privately owned aircraft maintained by the Bianchi family at Personal Plane Services).
Bücker Bü 131 Jungmann
Bücker Bü 133 Jungmeister
Comper Swift

Below: A particularly fine shot of the Shuttleworth Spitfire V, which is normally housed at Duxford.

Bottom right: Also owned by the Shuttleworth Collection is this stripped-down Avro Anson, a worthy subject for restoration, here seen in the Duxford engineering shop in 1976.

de Havilland Dragon Rapide
Fiat G.46
Fieseler Storch
Fokker E III Eindecker replica
Manning Flanders MF.1 Monoplane replica
Morane-Saulnier Type N replica
Morane-Saulnier MS 230
North American T-6
Percival Proctor
Piper J-3 Cub
Sopwith Triplane replica
Stampe/SE.5A replica
Supermarine Spitfire Mk 1a
Supermarine Spitfire Mk IX

Movieland of the Air, John Wayne Airport, Santa Ana, California.
Blériot XI
Curtiss Pusher
Fokker E III Eindecker
Maurice Farman
Nieuport 28
Sopwith Camel
SPAD S.VII
Sopwith Triplane
Fokker DR1 Triplane

Fokker D.7
Curtiss Jenny
Thomas-Morse S4B
Boeing P-12
Curtiss Gulfhawk
Grumman Duck
Curtiss P-40E Warhawk
North American B-25 Mitchell

Resident at Redhill, Surrey, is this Bücher Bü 133 Jungmeister formerly owned by James Gilbert and maintained in the authentic markings of the pre-war German sport flying organisation, Deutscher Luftsport Verband.

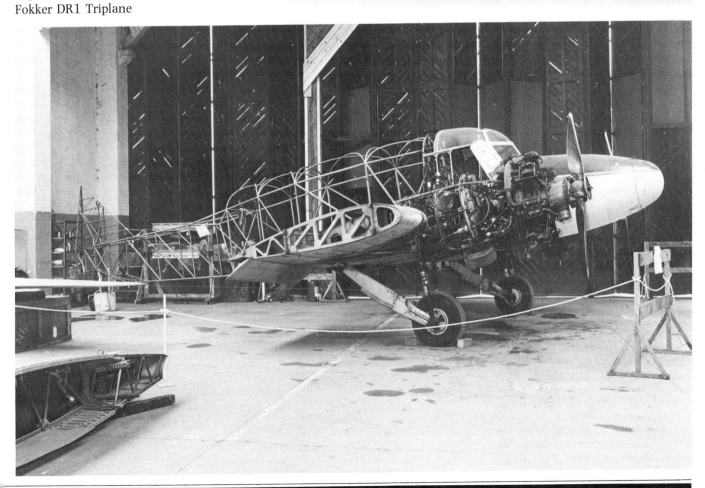

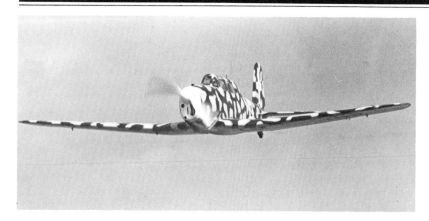

Top: This privately owned
Fiat G-46 basic trainer, a
type used by the Italian
Air Force from 1947, is
based at Booker in
Buckinghamshire.

Above: A regular visitor to
various airshow airfields
around the UK, though
based at Sywell, is this
privately owned Nord 1002
Pingouin, French-built
Messerschmitt Bf 108
Taifun four-seat sport and
communications aircraft.

Right: Several collections,
including the Blackbushe
and Movieland concerns
listed in this section,
maintain North American
B-25 Mitchells, the bomber/
ground attack aircraft made
famous by the Doolittle
carrier-based attack on
Tokyo. The CAF B-25
pictured is one of the rarer
'solid'-nosed marks
developed to carry a 75mm
cannon or eight machine-
guns for ground attack.

Left: With many still in service around the world, few collections include Douglas DC-2s or -3s or their various derivatives; yet having first flown in 1933 the type has a valid ranking as a flying antique. These two C-47 Skytrains maintained by the CAF acknowledge the major contribution made to World War II by the 10,000–plus military derivatives of the classic and timely Douglas design.

Below: One of the most-restored airworthy aeroplanes, and therefore to be seen in its natural element virtually every-where that antique aircraft still fly, is the ubiquitous North American AT-6 Texan, or Harvard with the RAF.

Above: Among the airworthy relics maintained by the Canadian National Museum of Science and Technology is this Nieuport 17, one of a range of the best of the World War I French fighters.

Left: Maintenance of originality and airworthiness is the aim of Drage's Aircraft Museum at Wodonga, Victoria, Australia, both achieved in this de Havilland Australia DH A3 Drover, one of three remaining examples of the 20 built.

Below left: Not only fixed-wing aircraft attract the enthusiastic restorer, as the attendance of this Piaseki H-21 helicopter at an Oshkosh fly-in attests. Piasecki Helicopter Corp, a pioneer of twin-rotor heavy-lift machines, became the present Boeing Vertol company, but its founder, Frank Piasecki, formed Piasecki Aircraft Corp in 1955 which is currently developing compound helicopters.

INDEX

ACKNOWLEDGEMENTS

Many people have contributed to this book both directly and indirectly over a number of years. To all of them go my thanks, especially to Captain Don Bullock of Euroworld Limited, Alan Chalkley, Don Ellis, the Fleet Air Arm Historic Flight, and Philip Wolf who generously provided their aircraft; to the Bianchi family at Personal Plane Services, Don Dwiggins in California, Stuart McKay of the De Havilland Moth Club, Merton Mead Jr of Shannon Air Museum, David Ogilvy of the Shuttleworth Trust, Cole Palen at Old Rhinebeck, and the late Neil

Williams for their assistance with information and photography; and to James Gilbert, Editor of *Pilot*, for permission to adapt certain passages originally written for the magazine.
Michael Jerram,
Southsea, Hampshire, February 1980

Air Portraits: 1, 10/11, 12/13, 14/15, 18 (top), 19 (top), 20/21, 24, 29 (top), 42, 43, 56 (top), 63 (top), 64/65, 105 (bottom), 125, 126, 140 (top), 147 (inset), 180/181 (all 3), 186, 187 (bottom).
Australian Information Service: 190

(centre).
Austin J Brown: 118/119, 139.
Canadian National Museum of Science and Technology: 41 (inset), 52, 57.
Don Dwiggins: 48/49 (all three), 88/89.
James Gilbert: 6/7, 17 (top & centre), 18/19 (bottom), 30/31 (main photo), 36/37, 38/39, 50/51 (top), 53 (top), 63 (bottom), 173 (inset), 175, 176 (top).
Stuart Howe: 17 (bottom), 132/133, 140 (centre), 156/157, 166, 167, 168/169 (top & bottom left), 170, 188/189 (centre top & bottom

left).
Inter-Air Press: 66 (top inset), 146 (inset), 184 (bottom).
Michael Jerram: Jacket 2/3, 22/23, 25 (both), 26/27 (bottom), 29 (bottom), 29 (bottom), 30/31 (top 2 left insets), 32/33, 34/35, 40/41, 44 (both), 46/47, 50/51 (bottom), 53 (bottom), 54/55, 56 (bottom), 58/59, 60/61, 62, 66/67, 68/69, 70/71, 72/73 (both), 74/75 (all 3), 77, 78, 79, 80/81 (both), 82/83, 86, 87, 93, 94/95, 96/97, 98/99, 101, 102/103, 104 (both), 105 (top), 106/107, 108/109 (main photo

& inset top right), 112/113, 116/117, 119 (inset), 122/123 (both), 127, 128, 129 (both), 131, 133 (inset), 134, 135, 141, 142/143 (both), 144, 145, 146/147 (main photo), 149, 150, 152/153, 155 (both), 158/159 (both), 160 (both), 161 (both), 164/165, 169 (bottom), 176 (centre), 178 (both), 185, 187 (top), 188 (top left 2), 189 (bottom), 190 (bottom).
Andy Keech: 110/111.
Ministry of Defence: 137 (inset); /HMS Heron: 162/163.
National Museum of Canada: 190

(top).
Old Rhinebeck Aerodrome: 8/9, 30/31 (top right inset); /Cole Palen: 4/5, 171, 174; via Philip Moyes: 172/173.
R E Richardson: 136/137, 183 (all 3), 184 (top).
Seenic Airlines: 85.
Hiroshi Seo: 90/91.
Shannon Air Museum: 179.
The Smithsonian Institute: 114/115.
USAAF: 121.
US Navy: 26 (top), 28 (both), 108 (inset).
Vought Corporation: 151.